"In *Desert Daughters, Desert So[...]*
of the Christian desert traditio[n...]
women in desert literature, and [...]
incisive analysis overturns norm[a...]
By employing the common category of offspring, Wheeler exposes a quest for
spiritual becoming grounded in community. Wheeler's approach and findings
are welcome; they merit examination and application in future scholarship.
This is a timely and important book."

> —Bernadette McNary-Zak
> Associate Professor of Religious Studies
> Rhodes College

"Those familiar with the *apophthegmata* of early monasticism will appreciate
Dr. Wheeler's close reading of the stories of monks' characterizations of
women, especially those that discount women so as to protect men's virtue.
Dr. Wheeler peers 'into the margins of the stories' and offers a much-needed
midrash and critique as invitations to read between the lines to present
alternative interpretations for readers, seeking wisdom and desiring
validation for living the Christian life today."

> —Mary Forman, OSB
> Prioress, Monastery of St. Gertrude, Idaho

"A beautiful, bold, and creative evocation of the representation and
experience of women in the world of early Christian monasticism. With
compassion, nuance, and courage, Rachel Wheeler offers us a feminist rereading of these early monastic traditions that is both liberating and healing.
Thanks to her painstaking scholarship and imaginative readings of the ancient
texts, we can now encounter the lives and voices of women who have too long
been obscured from view. But more than this, her work invites us to rethink
the meaning of the tradition as a whole. An original and important work."

> —Douglas E. Christie, PhD
> Professor, Department of Theological Studies
> Loyola Marymount University

"Rachel Wheeler explores the contradictions in a literature that can be so
moving and yet so jarring, focusing as it often did on the devaluing of
women and family relationships in a new ascetic social dynamic based on
spiritual fatherhood. Wheeler's creative deconstruction of these ancient texts
allows them to speak in a fresh voice while encouraging dialogue about their
embedded assumptions. This is precisely the kind of reading we need so that
classics of the monastic tradition can continue to inspire."

> —Fr. Columba Stewart, OSB, DPhil
> Executive Director
> Hill Museum & Manuscript Library, Collegeville, Minnesota

"In *Desert Daughters, Desert Sons*, Rachel Wheeler skillfully turns the ship of contemporary spiritual praxis with the twin rudders of creatively reading early Christian desert literature and critically applying theoretical considerations to the texts and characters of Christian late antiquity. Wheeler uncovers the hidden waters of women's voices and concerns that lie just under the surface of these dusty, male-centered texts, and in so doing floods the Egyptian desert with hidden communities necessary for spiritual formation—including forming oneself by oneself and allowing marginalized voices to form one's own journey. In piloting the reader through these waters, Wheeler invites contemporary practitioners of Christian spirituality to refract early Christian wisdom in ways that emphasize the necessities of community and women's voices, so long forgotten and underappreciated in the spiritual experience."

—Zachary B. Smith, PhD
    Associate Professor of Theology (History of Christianity) and
        faculty in the Women and Gender Studies Program
    Creighton University

"With *Desert Daughters, Desert Sons*, Rachel Wheeler gives us an always-needed rereading of the desert fathers and mothers portrayed in the *Apophthegmata Patrum* or *Sayings of the Desert Fathers*. With her close readings of sayings from the alphabetical, anonymous, and systematic sayings, she challenges assumptions, peers into the margins, and offers new insights into the 'peripheral women' in early-monastic stories and sayings. She re-stories the texts from a perspective that focuses with new insight mostly on the daughters of the desert."

—Tim Vivian
    Professor Emeritus of Religious Studies
    California State University Bakersfield

"According to a famous monastic saying, the ancient Egyptian desert was the place where 'there are no women.' But Rachel Wheeler shows that this was not and could not be so. In this thought-provoking study of desert spirituality, she invites us to turn our focus away from the solitary male heroes of monastic stories and notice the many women who inhabit the periphery of those stories or who become hauntingly present in their absence. By attending to desert daughters as well as desert sons, Wheeler uncovers the pain caused by distancing ourselves from one another, and she offers us a way of love, not only for those traveling alone in their deserts, but also for those seeking renewed community among men and women in cities, churches, and families."

—David Brakke
    The Ohio State University

Desert Daughters, Desert Sons

Rethinking the Christian Desert Tradition

Rachel Wheeler

LITURGICAL PRESS

Collegeville, Minnesota

www.litpress.org

1   2   3   4   5   6   7   8   9

Library of Congress Cataloging-in-Publication Data

Names: Wheeler, Rachel M., author.
Title: Desert daughters, desert sons : rethinking the Christian desert tradition / Rachel Wheeler.
Description: Collegeville, Minnesota : Liturgical Press, 2020. | Includes bibliographical references. | Summary: "In Desert Daughters, Desert Sons, Rachel Wheeler argues that a new reading of the texts of the Christian desert tradition is needed to present the (often) anonymous women who inhabit the texts"— Provided by publisher.
Identifiers: LCCN 2020014988 (print) | LCCN 2020014989 (ebook) | ISBN 9780814685006 (paperback) | ISBN 9780814685259 (epub) | ISBN 9780814685259 (mobi) | ISBN 9780814685259 (pdf)
Subjects: LCSH: Desert Fathers. | Monastic and religious life of women—History—Early church, ca. 30-600.
Classification: LCC BR67 .W44 2020 (print) | LCC BR67 (ebook) | DDC 270.2082—dc23
LC record available at https://lccn.loc.gov/2020014988
LC ebook record available at https://lccn.loc.gov/2020014989

Not understanding what has happened
prevents us from going on to something better.

—Poemen 200

Contents

Acknowledgments

I am grateful for the support of

- *mentors* Arthur Holder, Darleen Pryds, and Carol Dempsey, OP;

- *colleagues* Nina Henrichs-Tarasenkova, David Turnbloom, and Jon Stanfill;

- *writing friends* Shannon McAlister, Stephen King, OFM Conv, and Aline Gram Lewis;

- *writers of the desert tradition* Bernadette McNary-Zak, Lillian Larsen, and Mary Forman, OSB;

- and *members* of the Harrison, Wheeler, Yoder, Gores, Drysdale, Ramirez, Singer, and DiMartino families, especially my parents, Beverly and Nick Harrison.

You have all been present to me in extraordinary ways as I have read, studied, interpreted, and taught the desert sayings and I thank you for your companionship. I extend a very special thanks to Hans Christoffersen and Tara Durheim of Liturgical Press for helping me bring this work to print, and to Winston Wheeler, without whom I would have neither started nor completed this work.

Introduction

When I first began reading *The Sayings of the Desert Fathers and Mothers* over twenty years ago, I was delighted to find that their teachings and tales—though ancient—often resonated with my own contemporary situation. These sayings told of men and women who were involved in a meaningful quest for experience of God and who knew how to use their bodily lives wisely while regulating food and sleep, relationships and time, in ways that made them more available and attentive to experience of God. These were men and women, too, curiously akin to the desert lovers I was reading while working on a graduate degree in English. Writers like Mary Austin, Ann Zwinger, and Terry Tempest Williams were all writing movingly of life in the desert.[1]

As I delighted in these ancient Christian writings and their modern analogues, I eventually began to work on a graduate degree in theology and then a doctoral degree in spirituality, both of which allowed me to go deeper into the spirituality of the desert tradition. All this time, I kept looking for evidence of archaeologists and scholars seeking—and finding—more of the texts comprising a desert literature of early

---

1. See, for instance, Mary Austin, *The Land of Little Rain* (New York: Houghton, Mifflin and Company, 1903), Ann Zwinger, *The Mysterious Lands: A Naturalist Explores the Four Great Deserts of the Southwest* (New York: Dutton, 1989), Terry Tempest Williams, *Red: Passion and Patience in the Desert* (New York: Pantheon Books, 2001).

1

Christianity. In particular, I kept hoping for the discovery of more texts *about* and even *by women*. For, indeed, these kinds of texts were and still are in short supply. Though some ancient sources report thousands of women living in the late antique desert and in early monastic communities,[2] we seem to have tales of only a few. There were doubtless many more women we might have heard of and heard from, and I kept hoping for a long while that new *lives* and teachings of these women would surface. Women just as interesting and wise as the named desert mothers (or *ammas*) Syncletica, Sarah, and Theodora. Women just as innovative and adventurous in their personal and pilgrim lives as Macrina, Melania, and Egeria.

After a while, I checked my hopes, realizing with disappointment that, unfortunately, the gatekeepers to these women's lives were men unlikely to find such lives worth reporting about. I also checked my hopes for another reason: I began to notice that *The Sayings of the Desert Fathers and Mothers* were *full* of women. Though not center stage, they were in fact *there*. That I began to notice these women at all I owe to such important teachers as Dr. Mary Forman, OSB, and her teaching on desert *ammas*, to Dr. Barbara Green, OP, and her teaching on biblical wisdom and its feminine expression, and especially Dr. Darleen Pryds and her teaching on women's leadership and whose research on marginalized women in the Franciscan movement continues to inspire me.[3] These scholars and teachers, though not always pointing the light on the

2. *The Lives of the Desert Fathers: The Historia Monachorum in Aegypto*, trans. Norman Russell, CS 34 (Kalamazoo, MI: Cistercian Publications, 1981), 67.

3. The classes I had with these women were deeply formative of my academic and personal journeys. For Mary Forman's work on women in the desert tradition, see *Praying with the Desert Mothers* (Collegeville, MN: Liturgical Press, 2005). For Darleen Pryds's work on women in the Franciscan tradition, see *Women of the Streets: Early Franciscan Women and their Mendicant Vocation* (St. Bonaventure, NY: Franciscan Institute, 2010).

specific women this book will showcase, did much to make it possible for me to *see* what had previously been invisible to me, and what I imagine remains invisible for many readers of the desert Christian tradition today.

Though the body of literature making up the sources for the desert tradition may strike some readers as arcane, the reader is likely to find some wildly fascinating stories to draw and retain her interest, even when not looking for or noticing women in the text. One such story involves a man assisted by ants to counter a bug infestation initiated by the devil to get the man to leave his cell during a Lenten fast.[4] The collaboration of the natural world in helping this man keep to his sacred routine evokes possibilities for reading the desert literature through a "green" lens, and much more work in that direction remains to be done. More commonly, we find exemplary men sharing their material goods and their wisdom with one another, in continuity with the biblical ideals expressed in the early chapters of the Acts of the Apostles. It is these exemplary male figures who capture the interest of most scholars and teachers of the Christian desert tradition. Of course, in this body of literature, we find women as well appearing here and there as exemplars, but for the most part these women are not exemplars themselves but are visitors, friends, sisters, and mothers to the exemplary men. That this host of women never entirely disappears from the desert tradition is important to the contemporary reader, especially its female reader. These men were never entirely able to get away from women, as much as they might have desired, tried to, and led us to believe they *had*.

---

4. *The Anonymous Sayings of the Desert Fathers: A Select Edition and Complete English Translation,* trans. John Wortley (Cambridge: Cambridge University Press, 2013), 629–31. Subsequent sayings from this source are cited by number as indicated in Wortley's translation as in this case: (Anon 763).

The persistence of women in the desert literature is enlightening for what it suggests about the ways in which human beings optimally function. The persistent presence of women in the desert provides a countertext to the Neoplatonic belief that the spiritual life is "a flight of the alone to the Alone."[5] Instead, that the stories in the collections of desert sayings commonly record what is often depicted as interference from both named and anonymous women suggests a reality we cannot overlook. Whether audibly or not, these women spoke wisdom about the spiritual life that we still need to hear. They said to male friends and family members, and they continue to say to us: "None of us are meant to go it alone." They go on to say, "We are here to join you not in 'a life taking no pleasure in the things of earth,' (the phrase preceding Plotinus's words quoted above) but in the participatory event of becoming." Helpers and helped alike, these women and men might, alternatively, collaborate with one another in their spiritual maturing.

To understand these persistent women and to understand what the male collectors of the literature meant by allowing their peripheral presence to be recorded, we as readers need to enlist our openness, intuition, empathy, and creativity as we put aside what we may assume about this desert tradition and the monastic tradition it fed, and listen to it anew. To be the stalwart male adrift in the wilderness, pitting himself against and vanquishing its terrorizing solitude and his own demons, has been the aspiration of men as contemporary to us as Henry David Thoreau, Edward Abbey, and Chris McCandless.[6] But a different relationship to the process of spiritual formation,

---

5. Plotinus, *The Enneads*, 6.9.11

6. Henry David Thoreau, *Walden*; Edward Abbey, *Desert Solitaire: A Season in the Wilderness* (New York: Ballantine Books, 1971); Jon Krakauer, *Into the Wild* (New York: Villard Books, 1996). A recent feminist critique of the androcentrism of this wilderness impulse is provided by Abi Andrews, *The Word for Woman is Wilderness* (Columbus, OH: Two Dollar Radio, 2019).

to community's role in that process, and to our environments is possible if we listen to women. It is this book's task to call our attention to the voices of women in the desert sayings and to suggest ways that listening to them will offer an alternate vision for a way of living together characterized as a way of love.[7]

In this introduction, I describe the historical setting of desert spirituality and the sources we have for investigating this period. I next offer an explanation for why I have chosen to refer to the women and men of these stories as *desert daughters* and *desert sons* rather than with the more familiar terms, *desert mothers* and *desert fathers*. Though my terminology may never catch on and I do not mean for it to jettison a whole rich tradition of associations around the metaphorical engendering that spiritual companionship makes possible, my language *is* meant to function as a corrective against allowing our too-familiar words to cause us to forget that all these women and men themselves had *real*—that is, biological and not just socio-spiritual—mothers and fathers. To that end, they had specific (unchosen) individuals to whom they owed their personhood, biologically and socio-spiritually. Though it is natural to pick one's own spiritual mentors and models—we do it ourselves all the time—it is essential to remember and honor our origins. This book investigates why male desert Christians did this forgetting and dishonoring, and it appeals to the contemporary reader to question and challenge that gesture within an important movement in the early history of Christian spirituality. This book further appeals to the contemporary reader to seek alternate routes forward from a renewed understanding of the spiritual maturing these men and women sought, even when the means they used to realize this maturing may seem suspect to us.

---

7. This phrase draws implicitly from the work of Belgian feminist philosopher, psychoanalyst, and linguist Luce Irigaray, *The Way of Love*, trans. Heidi Bostic and Stephen Pluháček (New York: Continuum, 2002).

Historical Setting of Desert Spirituality

The Christian desert tradition originated with people expectant for the return of Christ and living in ways they felt were consistent with such expectation. By the middle of the third century, many Christian men and women were living in solitude away from what they considered the turmoil and distractions of urban life. Though not many could venture too far from vital sources of food and water, the desert held an allure for being both a literal place of retreat for these Christians as well as a place representing (metaphorically) the Christian's own recalcitrant, uncivilized soul in need of reform.[8] The image of "working the earth of one's heart"[9] for the harvest of the seed of the Word (referring to Scripture and to Christ) drew both from biblical narratives as well as the everyday life experience of many who worked the land to provide food for themselves, their families, and others—always, of course, close enough to the Nile River or some other such water supply to maintain their gardens or fields.

The way of Christian life that emerged from this time and place has come to be known as desert spirituality. Thomas Merton writes, "The real desert is this: to face the real limitations of one's own existence and knowledge and not to manipulate them or disguise them. Not to embellish them with possibilities."[10]

---

8. For a lovely evocation of the desert's biblical symbolism and significance for early Christians, see Eucherius of Lyons, "In Praise of the Desert," trans. Charles Cummings, in *The Lives of the Jura Fathers*, ed. Tim Vivian, Kim Vivian, and Jeffrey Burton Russell, CS 178 (Kalamazoo, MI: Cistercian Publications, 1999), 197–215.

9. A phrase attributed to Pseudo-Macarius and the evocative title of Columba Stewart's study of the Messalian controversy, *Working the Earth of the Heart: The Messalian Controversy in History, Texts, and Language to A.D. 431* (Oxford: Clarendon Press, 1991).

10. Thomas Merton, *Learning to Love: Exploring Solitude and Freedom*, The Journals of Thomas Merton Volume Six (New York: HarperCollins, 2010), 309. Cited in Belden C. Lane, *The Great Conversation: Nature and the Care of the Soul* (New York: Oxford University Press, 2019), 132.

Desert spirituality refers to a way of Christian life characterized by opportunities made possible to the Christian believer by the presence of desert, whether literal or metaphorical. In the former case, the actual place of the desert often meant a person experienced deprivation as a significant aspect of their material and spiritual existence—deprivation of vital resources like food and water, the company of others, adequate sleep, and time to devote to commercial success. These were not necessarily seen as *bad* deprivations by the desert Christian community, but rather seen as opening up the Christian adapting to these material realities to new forms of experience, new apprehensions of the human self and of God. Similarly, the metaphorical desert meant that even Christians living among others in an urban center might curtail their involvement with material possessions and resources in order to simulate the experience of deprivation that those in the actual deserts experienced. This kind of life can be seen as contiguous with the emerging monastic paradigms of the fourth and later centuries.

Tradition focuses on the figure of Antony of Egypt as the first of these men and women who ventured into desert solitude.[11] In his early twenties, he heard Scripture read in church calling him to an act of radical conversion and renunciation. Leaving a sister behind for whom he was responsible—a poignant detail—Antony first made the rounds of wise elders near his home to learn from them what he could. He was, as his biographer Athanasius puts it, like a bee picking up sweets

11. Athanasius, *The Life of Antony*, trans. Robert C. Gregg, Classics of Western Spirituality (New York: Paulist Press, 1980). To be fair, the emerging desert tradition did provide what seems to be *alternate* resources for women. For instance, the attribution of "Pseudo-Athanasius" to the authorship of *The Life of Syncletica* indicates an intentional parallel being established between Antony and a female counterpart in the person of Syncletica, who was also based in Egypt and also responsible for a female sibling in the early part of her story. See Pseudo-Athanasius, *The Life and Regimen of the Blessed and Holy Syncletica*, trans. Elizabeth Bryson Bongie (Eugene, OR: Wipf and Stock, 2005).

from various flowers. Having sampled all the teachings of the elders surrounding his location, he wove of these teachings a rule for himself to live alone in an abandoned fortress, also not too far from his home. There, friends might visit him to bring food or to check that he had not yet died of boredom or fasting or combat with evil forces. After a long while so sequestered, Antony is said to have emerged transformed. His time in the solitary cell served as a crucible in which he was crushed, or as a womb from which he emerged anew—a metaphor deserving further attention. He retreated at this point further into the desert, finding what was called his Inner Mountain, a home he loved where he might plant a garden and eat the fruits of a palm tree for his physical sustenance. Many, having heard reports of his transformation, sought him out as an exemplar of the countercultural life he represented: a quasi-solitary life, not supporting the Roman Empire by virtue of economic or social participation. Antony did not buy or sell, did not marry, did not father children, did not in fact participate fully in the emerging rites of the Christian church.[12] Much of this, of course, represented a substantial threat to the Empire if too many of its citizens followed suit, and a threat to the early faith communities and their own centers of episcopal authority. Over time as this type of lifestyle became exemplary within Christian faith communities, the solitaries won respect in adjudicating difficult cases and serving an important social function for various communities,[13] despite or rather because of their solitary lifestyle—non-affiliated with any one person or group, and considered thus impartial.

12. One of the most important contemporary interpreters of the desert Christians' countercultural activities is Belden C. Lane. See, for instance, his *Desert Spirituality and Cultural Resistance: From Ancient Monks to Mountain Refugees* (Eugene, OR: Wipf and Stock, 2018).

13. Peter Brown, "The Rise and Function of the Holy Man in Late Antiquity," *Journal of Roman Studies* 61 (1971): 80–101.

By the time of St. Benedict in the late fifth and early sixth centuries, many dedicated Christians, forgoing familial life for the pleasures of solitude had set up their hermitages and communities throughout North Africa, Israel, Turkey, Syria, Italy, France, Spain, and England. The third and fourth centuries, however, saw these ascetic Christians creating lives primarily *in the deserts* of Egypt, Palestine, and Syria. At times, stories in the collections of desert sayings depict these revered men and women in contact with church leaders, often to provide a foil of sorts to the church-bound Christian dedicated to the "worldly" business of the faith community.[14] These kinds of stories promote the desert Christians as more attuned to divine presence because of their non-investment of time and energy in organized religious life. It can be argued that this idealistic divide between the so-called desert fathers and mothers and Christian bishops is simply that: idealistic. Yet the stories emerging to support the desert lifestyle use almost every opportunity they can to highlight the superiority of the desert life as an authentic, if not the *most* authentic, expression of imitation of Christ. After all, Scripture records how Jesus retreated often to the wilderness to pray (see, for instance, Luke 4:42; 5:16). When, in rare cases, a bishop is seen as equal to a desert Christian or even superior to a desert Christian—this serves as a lesson for cultivating humility among the stories' characters and their later avid monastic readers.[15]

14. For a thorough study of the late antique bishop, see Claudia Rapp, *Holy Bishops in Late Antiquity: The Nature of Christian Leadership in an Age of Transition* (Berkeley: University of California Press, 2005). Rapp's book reminds us of the overlap of ascetic figures and bishops in this period, so that a clear distinction between the two is propagandistic.

15. See, for example, the exchange between Epiphanius and Hilarion in *The Book of the Elders: Sayings of the Desert Fathers*, trans. John Wortley, CS 240 (Collegeville, MN: Liturgical Press, 2012), 41. Subsequent citations from this source will be cited within the text with chapter name and saying number in parentheses as in this case: (Self-Control 15). Used by permission.

Certainly, however removed from ecclesial politics the desert Christians are represented as being, their own internal politics were taking shape.[16] Their own organization and rules were quickly evolving and leaders to enforce such rules were emerging that accrued their own authority among the desert Christians. Why did this happen? In part, because those involved in forming these early spiritual communities could understand their rules of life and their leaders as forming *them* after the pattern of Christ. They experienced in others a forming of the person of Christ, what they saw as an authentic enactment of Christian discipleship, which they wanted to implement in their own lives. Following the same rules and leaders as others allowed them to further their own spiritual development. Eventually, these patterns of holiness attracted pilgrims and imitators, and they affected the Christian community more globally.

Indeed, for women, the first centuries of the Common Era created an oasis of freedom when they might legitimately choose not to marry and have children so as to dedicate themselves, just as men could, to a relationship with God in a supportive community that valued similar things. Setting up what we might suspect is a false dichotomy between spiritual and social life, these women were confirmed in their decision to not have families or to not remarry once widowed, and their restraint from sexual activity became an important factor in legitimizing their otherwise-suspect spiritual authority. When spiritual men's exemplarity rested on an ability to harness their physical energies in ways that women could do as well, asceti-

16. Many studies of this developmental period in Christian history exist. See, as an example, Derwas J. Chitty, *The Desert a City: An Introduction to the Study of Egyptian and Palestinian Monasticism under the Christian Empire* (Crestwood, NY: St. Vladimir's Seminary Press, 1999). Chitty draws his title from the classic text, *The Life of Antony*, in which the image of "city" is used to begin speaking of the communities formed in the desert.

cism of the body became an equalizing force. This will have its own problems when we consider the ascetic competitiveness that seems to have arisen from this situation in the history of Christianity.

For the moment, it is useful to note that the desert movement provided a unique means for women's spiritual transformation and was attractive thus as a means by which women might cultivate their own relationship with God, independent of men's supervision. Other moments in the history of Christian spirituality similarly show this female autonomy as possible, but this early period has pride of place as being the first to elaborate, in practice, the significance of Paul's words, "There is neither . . . male nor female" (Gal 3:28). Gendered identity did not disqualify a person from fruitfully engaging in ascetic and contemplative practices and making oneself available to the experience of being fully present to oneself, to others, and to God. As we shall see, however, our sources from this period deal with this reality of gender equality in troubled and troubling ways.

Desert Literature: A Survey of Sources

Stories of these women and men are found in various literary sources from this late antique period, as well as into the early medieval period. These early sources present such stories in varying genres, such as the *lives* or biographies of the desert Christians, early church histories, treatises on prayer and ascetic life, and collections of pithy sayings. We even find the tenth century dramatist Hrotsvitha of Gandersheim writing plays about the desert Christians! Of course, all of these literary forms have their own conventional rules, agenda, means of persuasion, and intended audience that their authors were keeping in mind when using the textual form to communicate tales and teachings of the desert. A brief survey of these early literary sources is as follows:

The *lives* or biographies of exemplary desert Christians were written by pilgrims who had visited them or heard about them. Not strictly biographical in nature, these works had a specific agenda: to promote the ascetic life through particular attention on spectacular feats, and to present the biographical material as evidence for a person's sanctity. The particular good works or miracles done by the person were to awe the reader first and then to persuade the reader to virtuous emulation.[17] *Histories* of legendary desert ascetics were similarly assembled by pilgrims and also by people who began to live like the legendary ascetics themselves either alone or in communities. These people drew inspiration from those whom they had visited or heard about and whom they considered pioneers in the lifestyle they were adopting themselves.[18] *Treatises* on ascetic practice and contemplative prayer authored by the desert elders themselves are important sources providing us with a look at the behaviors most valued by these figures and their circles of disciples. They provide us with firsthand knowledge of the problems and solutions most experienced by those who set themselves up to live ostensibly alone with God.[19] Lastly,

17. Examples include the previously mentioned *Life of Anthony* by Athanasius; Pseudo-Athanasius's *The Life and Regimen of the Blessed and Holy Syncletica*, trans. Elizabeth Bryson Bongie (Eugene, OR: Wipf and Stock, 2005); and "Life of Pelagia," etc., in Benedicta Ward's *Harlots of the Desert: A Study of Repentance in Early Monastic Sources*, CS 106 (Kalamazoo, MI: Cistercian Publications, 1987).

18. Examples include the previously mentioned *Lives of the Desert Fathers* or *Historia Monachorum in Aegypto* and Palladius's *Lausiac History*, trans. Robert T. Meyer, ACW 34 (Mahwah, NJ: Paulist Press, 1964).

19. Examples include Evagrius Ponticus, *The Praktikos and Chapters on Prayer*, trans. John Eudes Bamberger, CS 4 (Collegeville, MN: Cistercian Publications, 1972); John Cassian, *Institutes*, trans. Boniface Ramsey, ACW 58 (Mahwah, NJ: Newman, 2000); and Isaiah of Scetis, *Ascetic Discourses*, trans. John Chryssavgis and Pachomios Penkett, CS 150 (Kalamazoo, MI: Cistercian Publications, 2002).

collections of short anecdotes and teachings (known simply as "sayings") emerged as people shared reports of stories heard from others. Each compilation of sayings differed slightly as the compilers made decisions both concerning *what* to include and *how* to organize its contents.[20] Though the lives, histories, and treatises of the desert Christians are well-worth investigation and will be referenced intermittently in this text,[21] principally I draw from the last type of source mentioned. *The Sayings of the Desert Fathers and Mothers* is the most varied, surprising, and interesting of these late antique texts on early Christian life. Because its stories were communicated first orally and then set down in writings to be ruminated over, the sayings collections had to contain work that was personal, pithy, and profound enough to catch and retain the interest of the storytellers and those who listened to these stories.

Indeed, the desert sayings are *personal* in that they relate what real people seem to have found interesting either to read, meditate upon, share with others, and retell in infinite variety, each repetition of a story or teaching revealing just as much about the person who told it as it does about the characters, stylized as they might eventually have become, in the story. The sayings are also *pithy* in that in order to be retained in memory for personal meditation and imitation, the stories had to be told in a precise, condensed form—allowing the hearer to perceive almost immediately what was the story's importance and to remember it. The sayings are, in addition, *profound* in their condensing wisdom in a proverbial sort of way, applicable to many situations though originally deriving from

20. See John Moschos, *Spiritual Meadow*, trans. John Wortley, CS 139 (Kalamazoo, MI: Cistercian Publications, 1992), in addition to the other collections I mention below.

21. An important reference book for study of these types of literature is William Harmless's *Desert Christians: An Introduction to the Literature of Early Monasticism* (New York: Oxford University Press, 2004).

a unique person's unique problem or query. In sometimes poetic, often short statements these desert sayings express an understanding of the natural world as humankind might learn from it, often framing such teachings with the words "just so . . . " linking observation of the natural world with the listeners' own protomonastic lifestyle. The statements also express an understanding of God that drew from personal experience, experience that was troubling or worth celebrating. The statements express both the distress and joys involved in coming to know more deeply one's own foibles and potential. Moreover, the sayings collections host a diverse assortment of peripheral characters, men and women, animals and rivers, trees and stones. This book focuses on the women among these peripheral characters, but just by virtue of being such a huge assortment of individual tales and teachings, the collections of desert sayings are a unique and worthy source for exploring early Christian experience and spirituality.

The background of the sayings genre seems to have been the *chreia*, deriving from the Socratic circles as disciples of wise men condensed pithy sayings of their masters to remember and use.[22] The word *chreia* evokes the Greek for "useful" and reminds us that this approach to memorizing teachings was not arbitrary or to uphold the masters' exemplary wise words, but rather for the listener to preserve in their memory and heart, and eventually embody in their own actions. Thus, the statement itself and the collecting of the statements into various collections had an explicit purpose: to be *used* as "equipment for living"[23] to effect a change in a person's religious experience and understanding, ethical response to troubling situations, and spiritual transformation.

---

22. *The Chreia in Ancient Rhetoric: The Progymnasmata*, eds. Ronald F. Hock and Edward N. O'Neil (Atlanta, GA: Scholars Press, 1986), 9.

23. Kenneth Burke's phrase. See his treatment of proverbs in his *The Philosophy of Literary Form: Studies in Symbolic Action*, Third Edition (Berkeley and Los Angeles: University of California Press, 1973), 293–304.

Three significant collections of these sayings emerged about the desert mothers/daughters and desert fathers/sons living during the third, fourth, and fifth centuries. The Alphabetical Collection,[24] as might be obvious from its name, presents stories alphabetically according to the desert son or desert daughter's name about whom the story is told. This collection has an advantage over the others, as its assembly of sayings under a particular name sometimes allows the reader to discern a distinct personality arising from stories attributed to Antony, for instance, or Arsenius, or Poemen, or Syncletica. It is sometimes as if the collected sayings under a specific name compose themselves a miniature *life* of a particular desert Christian. Similarly, at times the advice offered from a specific desert elder can be seen to comprise a mini-rule of life. However, a distinct disparity between genders is obvious when surveying the inclusion of only three named women in contrast to the 128 named men whose stories and teachings are contained in this collection. This imbalance may be thought to represent the unbalanced numbers of real men and women in the Christian deserts, and yet they seemingly do not. Other documents, such as the *Historia Monachorum*, record huge numbers of women as part of what is often thought of as the protomonastic movement of this time. The imbalance is more likely explained as evidence of men's disregard for the importance of women's stories, evidence that will be further explored as we engage specific stories in the sayings collections.

Another collection, called the Anonymous Collection,[25] presents an assortment of stories with unknown derivation,

24. *The Sayings of the Desert Fathers: The Alphabetical Collection*, trans. Benedicta Ward, CS 59 (Kalamazoo, MI: Cistercian Publications, 1984); *Give Me a Word: The Alphabetical Sayings of the Desert Fathers*, trans. John Wortley (Yonkers, NY: St. Vladimir's Seminary Press, 2014).

25. *The Anonymous Sayings of the Desert Fathers: A Select Edition and Complete English Translation*, trans. John Wortley (Cambridge: Cambridge University Press, 2013).

though many stories in this text do refer to named individuals, as well. The Systematic Collection,[26] the most comprehensive of the three collections, is organized by themes such as discernment, love, and obedience. Much as biblical scholars have compared and contrasted material included in the four gospels, scholars of the collections of *apophthegmata* (or sayings) have noted duplication of stories between collections and inclusion of unique material in different collections. Though many of the genres of early Christian literature are useful for understanding more about the Christian desert tradition, this book will draw mostly from these sayings collections as they contain a host of women easily identifiable as peripheral or marginalized and whose stories have not been recognized, told, or interpreted in other scholarly texts.

Reading these sayings collections responsibly means we take into account their motley character, keeping in mind that though inclusion of some stories and the values they enshrine may seem opaque to us now, the collections functioned as keepsake reminders to their owners and original readers of the kind of life one aspired to oneself. Thus, their contents reveal what some people thought exemplary at some time. Conversely, the contents themselves were responsible in part for cultivating a sensibility among early monastic readers of just what was exemplary. This situation reveals itself as a two-way street, a closed system perhaps that we will try to break into with this book. Was it quite necessary that certain behaviors came to be considered holier than others, affecting not only late antique and early medieval sensibilities but even formative of our own religious assumptions in the twenty-first century? Was it quite necessary that certain people came to be considered holier than others, and certain actions more conducive to the cultivation of holiness than others? Was it quite neces-

---

26. *The Book of the Elders: Sayings of the Desert Fathers*, trans. John Wortley, CS 240 (Collegeville, MN: Liturgical Press, 2012).

sary that the path to spiritual perfection often lay through the devastated lives of marginalized women?

Because some of the peripheral women considered in this book provide other possibilities for creation and understanding of the holy, the revered, and the exemplary, it will be necessary to check our first impulse in reading these stories as they have been read ever since their assembly into organized collections. We will need to read responsibly *and* creatively with a hermeneutic derived in part from Elisabeth Schüssler Fiorenza's work on the New Testament, which she describes as a "creative hermeneutic." She employs this creative hermeneutic in biblical studies to imaginatively reconstruct the lives of New Testament women and women in early faith communities.[27] We can do the same here with women a few centuries later. To do so means we consider possibilities about the lives of these women without shutting down options due to what we have likely been taught to believe about Christian tradition and what constitutes virtue and what constitutes sanctity. And, like Schüssler Fiorenza, we do this not primarily to understand the past better—if indeed we can be understood to do this at all. Instead, we do it for the liberating vision it offers us to reassess what is our present reality and to reimagine what might be our future.

Why Desert Daughters, Desert Sons?

Why bother investigating gendered language, identities, relationships, and assumptions in the Christian desert tradition? After all, some of the best kernels of wisdom found in the

27. Elisabeth Schüssler Fiorenza, *Wisdom Ways: Introducing Feminist Biblical Interpretation* (Maryknoll, NY: Orbis Books, 2001), 179–83, 202. See also Alice Connor, *Fierce: Women of the Bible and Their Stories of Violence, Mercy, Bravery, Wisdom, Sex, and Salvation* (Minneapolis, MN: Fortress, 2017) for a good example of both critical analysis and creative engagement with stories of women in the Bible.

sayings collections contain no reference to gender at all. For instance, my favorite desert saying is one found in the second chapter of the Systematic Collection and one I use frequently when introducing others to contemplative prayer or mindfulness meditation. To nearly anyone desiring practice of being wholly attentive to the presence of God and to what God is doing in their lives, this brief teaching continues to speak:

> In the same way that no plant whatsoever grows up on a well-trodden highway, not even if you sow seed, because the surface is trodden down, so it is with us. Withdraw from all business into *hēsychia* [or quietness] and you will see things growing that you did not know were in you, for you were walking on them. (Hesychia 33)

Like other wise and useful sayings, this saying draws from personal observation of the natural world and models the kind of correlation made often by the desert elders between features of their natural environment and the inner workings of their lives. Further, like other wise sayings, this saying appeals to no gendered identity to perform. You need be neither man nor woman, specifically, to feel invited to or excluded from applying this teaching to your own experience. If anything, the saying marginalizes those crippled or unable to walk while drawing on and privileging the experience of walkers, communicating to those able to walk as able to understand experientially the inadvertent tromping down of seedlings underfoot on a well-worn path.

Nevertheless, many of the sayings operate from an explicit identification of the speaker as male, speaking most often to other men of his acquaintance. This communication of wisdom between master and disciple as a specifically gendered activity excluding women will be examined in later sections of this book. At this point, I want solely to comment on the common designation of these "masters" of the spiritual life in the Christian desert as desert fathers and desert mothers. These are not only gendered identifications but assume *engendering* as a metaphorical function or exchange between (most often male) master and disciple. It is necessary to address both the benefits and drawbacks of using such language.

The exemplary men and women of the Christian desert have traditionally been known as desert fathers and desert mothers, respectively. These names are beautiful expressions of the endearing quality of relationship disciples felt they had with these exemplary, wise people. Age did not always matter in such identifications as a young person might be known as *elder* merely by virtue of his exemplary wisdom. Indeed, some stories make a point of making this identification of such a young person, because of the cultural assumptions concerning the wisdom of the aged that such an identification reveals.[28] Such resistance of a cultural assumption often builds, as well, upon the "wise child" motif in ancient literature[29] and the Bible itself (Luke 2:41-52). Ordinarily, wisdom might seem to belong to those who have lived long and experienced many things. Those who were well-practiced in the spiritual life adopted by men and women in the desert and could communicate well with others about how to practice such a life themselves were known as desert fathers and desert mothers.

Speaking one's reverence for a beloved elder teacher by calling them father or mother indicates hierarchy, but of a kind we likely tolerate and may even find appealing. The one who uses this identification uses it to reflect their own more vulnerable, needy status as one who requires the nourishment and guidance a parental figure can offer. This self-identification has its benefits in helping a person realize their fundamental origin in and reliance on another, a situation allowing them

28. See, for instance, Poemen 61 and Anon 451.

29. Alison Goddard Elliott, *Roads to Paradise: Reading the Lives of the Early Saints* (Hanover, NH: University Press of New England, 1987), 77–80.

to understand and live fully the truths that "I exist because of you. You brought me into being. Because of you, I continue to have being." The person to whom one can say such things naturally assumes a valued position.

These statements of truth are quite profound, and they explain why parental imagery is used of God throughout the Hebrew and Christian Scriptures. It explains, too, why many religious people refer to ordained male clergy in their own faith communities as "Father." It also, of course, raises problematic issues which this book's title is at pains to uncover. These revered figures themselves had filial loyalties that they often disregarded when achieving the status of "parent" to another. Further, by rendering one childlike in response to a revered elder, language of "fatherhood" or "motherhood" serves to maintain a person's dependence on another person indefinitely rather than evoke the reality that eventually children grow up and, if healthy, they move on with their own lives and establish their own independence. This fact of human social existence and development is rarely factored into representations of spiritual relationship in the desert tradition. So, while it is important to acknowledge the authority and generative value of progenitors in the faith, it is also important to recognize what facts of human spiritual maturation are obscured and even prevented by such language.

Not only is a disciple's dependence on another person and failure to think of himself or herself as capable of maturing signified by desert "father" and desert "mother" language, another failure inscribed in the language is the misdirection of generation from one's biological father and mother. This transfer from literal to spiritual parenthood is significant in that it highlights an important—highly problematic—redefinition of value. When a person's fidelity is reallocated away from the familial to an adopted familial context, the collapse of the literal familial context is imminent. Hardly anyone in the desert tradition takes account of the severed relationships necessary to facilitate spiritual relationships, which remains a "problem" that has not gone away and may never go away.

Strategies of Identification

Many contemporary scholars of the desert tradition have responded to these problems by using the gender-neutral "elder" or "desert Christian" to speak of both desert fathers and mothers. These terms suggest the identity of these wise figures without obscuring their other familial relations and obligations. While I like and use these words frequently myself, it is my desire to experiment in this book with the terms desert *daughter* and desert *son* as these terms allow me to highlight the recurrent obscuring of fidelity away from biological mother to spiritual father. The privileging of male spiritual progenitors over the physical maternal progenitor has allowed many men to dismiss the presence of women in their lives for the companionship of other men. The dismissal of such women has impoverished these men's lives rather than rendered them more free to resist tempting thoughts spawned by memories of beloved ones. This transfer of loyalty has allowed men and women both to conveniently forget an important fact of their existence: that their physical mothers, bearing them in their bodies for nine months and delivering them with much pain and joy, brought them into existence and reared them. The love and affection prompted by these figures' engendering is not negligible. A simple truth is evident here: each desert father had a mother and was thus a desert son. Each desert mother had a mother and was thus a desert daughter.

While certainly not everybody has affectionate feelings toward family members, we can hardly imagine that all desert fathers and mothers, and subsequent people who use language of family members to speak of authority figures in their faith communities, come from broken or disturbed homes that need replacing by better representatives. It would be interesting, of course, to know if the movement in this direction was begun by somebody or a group of people who did want to replace bad or failed biological relationships with better spiritual ones. In Antony's case, the death of his parents precipitated a movement away from his remaining sibling, a sister, so as to live independently. Whether or not this was the case with other influential Christians of this period, we do not know. Being orphaned would not have been an unusual experience in a time when warfare and disease curtailed the longevity of human life. But the persistence of replacement with a metaphorical family for one's own surviving biological family members will be something this book seeks to condemn—especially when it led to the entrenched patriarchal quality of contemporary Christian experience.

Replacement of biological relationships usurped the rights of mothers especially to be revered in their own maternity. Indeed, a too heavy dualism is inscribed in this splitting of biological and spiritual, as if the biological could not convey teachings appropriate to spiritual life, and the spiritual could not convey teachings appropriate to biological life. My use of *desert sons* and *desert daughters* to speak of individuals in the Christian desert tradition redresses this dualistic imbalance. While I hardly mean to infantilize these figures within the desert literature, I do mean to remind the reader of the sonhood and daughter-hood of all, including revered figures in Christian history who, even if they achieved the status of spiritual progenitor, still themselves remained men and women born of others. Being born of others is a key movement in not only one's biological life but in the initiation into a spiritual community made up of biological relationships and kinship with all creation. Indeed, to speak of *desert* daughter and *desert* son, I mean also to evoke the engendering aspect of the desert setting itself in which these characters' spiritual lives flourished, as it too facilitated ongoing births of their renewed beings, begun by a physical mother and assisted in numerous ways by mentors of all sorts. Responsive to the elements around them, whether the dry or wet seasons, to the opportunities to build homes from clay or rock, to draw sustenance from water reservoirs and fruiting trees, the desert Christians lived lives of spirit embedded within a natural world that shaped their experience and growth—just as the harsh desert winds would shape the face of the earth.

A final thought about this obscuring of motherhood in the desert sayings by focus on the spiritual father: the names we have for these men are various, such as Moses, Macarius, Poemen, Evagrius, and so on. Many of them may be representative or have special status as a name that indicates something important about a spiritual leader in the desert. For instance, the name "Poemen" simply indicates "shepherd." Though one story indicates Poemen's status as a young "wise child" consulting an old man about thoughts and being approved for his consultation by the old man's connecting his name with "shepherd of the flock" (Poemen 1), it is impossible to know whether this name may have been more an honorific than a name given this man (or several men known by this title) at birth. We have few ceremonies, if any, of name changes at this period, though that would become common with monastic profession in later centuries. The names then preserved in all likelihood for these men and the ones by which we know these men are those given by their parents. Imagine the mother of the desert son Moses as a Jewish or Christian woman naming her child after one of Israel's most impressive leaders. Imagine the mother of the desert son Macarius the Egyptian or Macarius the Alexandrian naming her child "blessed" either as her own special blessing for the child's life or to indicate her own special joy in bringing forth life. Though there may seem an unfair imbalance of distribution of men and women in the desert sayings, behind every man, as the saying goes, is a mother and a father, the former being our particular focus in this book.

Organization of the Book

The book will begin with a chapter that "makes space" for contemporary female readers of the Christian desert tradition by shining a light on three assumptions that typically shape interpretation of this key movement in the early history of Christian spirituality. These three assumptions have to do with expectations about the readership of the Christian desert tradition (that is, who the literature is for), about the exemplary hierarchical relationship between master and disciple (that is, how spiritual growth happens through communication between teacher and student, both typically male), and about the exemplary quality of a received teaching (that is, where wisdom resides). Having acknowledged these assumptions and explored their implications for useful reading of the Christian desert tradition today, we will then be able to move a bit more comfortably in our investigations of the sayings.

Chapter two documents some of the most perplexing and vexing sayings for women readers: particularly those having to do with men's anxiety toward, phobia about, or even hatred of women. When we consider the gospel tradition of Jesus's example of singling out those capable of hating family members as worthy disciples (Luke 14:26), we can begin to see what motivated these early Christians who intentionally removed themselves from proximity to family members, focusing on withdrawal from female family members (whether mothers, sisters, wives, or daughters), and begin to see why these women symbolized for men a kind of obstacle to the life of Christian discipleship they wished to design for themselves. Representing the desert thus lacking in women's presence is, however, wishful thinking on the part of these men, for women certainly were making their own journeys to places beyond those circumscribed for them by familial and cultural settings, and existing as neighbors to these men in the desert.

Chapter three considers women's "disappearance" into the discourse exchanged by men in the Christian desert tradition, looking specifically at sayings that show how women's ephemeral presence in the desert was relegated to metaphor. The specific metaphors we will focus on are those for the soul and for *hesychia*, the desired stillness of body and spirit that the desert environment seemed uniquely to make possible. As we trace this so-called "disappearance" of women from the literal landscape of the desert into the conversation exchanged by men into particularly valued aspects of their experience, we can see a lauding of the female but only a superficial lauding, as the real woman has had to be camouflaged or excised from the desert discourse to emerge, replaced by metaphor. Traces of real women exist, of course, but the most valued were those who proved competitors to the male ascetics, who used women's existence in the desert instrumentally to their own advantage as measurements by which they might better prove themselves to themselves, to others, and to God. In this third chapter, I further consider the significance of using the language of desert "father" and desert "mother" to speak of spiritual genealogy. As I have already noted, as profound as this language is to convey what a spiritual director makes possible for a directee, the language usurps the reality of physical engendering, of honoring the real mothers and fathers from whom the desert daughters and sons received their own being. Such language also will be seen to obscure the influence of multiple factors related to spiritual growth, including the desert itself as place of habitation.

Chapters four and five both provide further evidence of women's having never really disappeared from the desert context, though an attempt seems to have been made by men to confine them to metaphors within linguistic exchange. Chapter four thus celebrates the women in the Christian desert tradition who captured the interest of their male counterparts through successfully adopting what men proposed as the ideal way of life for early Christian ascetics, though very few of these women actually made their way into the literature about the desert tradition. It is undeniable that many women achieved remarkable success in their spiritual lives and helped many others as a result of deciding not to marry and have children. Asceticism could be, for them, liberating and transformative. However, I characterize this success in winning men's admiration as questionable when it reduced women's ways of life to duplication of men's ways of life and prohibited women from fostering their own physical, cultural, and spiritual becoming and well-being. Stories of this kind of success will have to be looked through as well, just as the stories expressing male anxiety, phobia, and hatred of women, for they only questionably represent what we can know of the women of the Christian desert tradition. In short, though it is significant to find at least three named women among those responsible for uttering sayings, this type of desert daughter, because of her duplication of masculine ascetic ideals, does not always represent the type of woman who might have modeled a spiritual life appropriate for women readers of this literature today. Without disowning her, however, we will try to look at how this woman has been depicted in the literature to trace out the depth of her life experience for what it might have meant for other women, besides being upheld as a model competitor for men.

A final chapter examines who these women might be who were the *real* desert mothers, sisters, daughters, and friends, and examines their experiences of loss and grief as their family members and friends chose to sever familial and other social relationships to take company with like-minded "brothers" or "sisters" under the leadership of a desert "father" or "mother." As Benedicta Ward writes in introducing us to the desert elder Poemen in her translation of the sayings, "The close ties of Egyptian monks with their families and their villages were constantly having to be broken in favour of the

freedom of the desert."[30] Ward's phrase "having to be" is
especially poignant. Who determined such a route to spiritual
freedom? And why did such a route have to lie through the
devastated lives of family members? Further, the "constantly
having to be" indicates an uneasiness with this emerging value
as men faced opportunities to reconnect with families and
villages and felt compelled to resist that reconnection: Who
determined that this must have been so? These are questions
that this book addresses. Rather than focus on these female
family members' lives as expressive of loss, grief, and tragedy,
however, I seek to recover their spirituality and wisdom as
they persisted as witnesses to another way of Christian life. We
will thus be able to imagine by focusing on these women's
experiences another direction in which Christian discipleship
might have developed—and might continue to develop today.
Alongside the kind of destructive work this book proposes to
do in explaining what seems to have been so threatening about
women's spirituality to men of this time period, the book will
propose a vision characterized as a *way of love* that derives from
the actions and persistent presence of marginalized women in
the Christian desert tradition.

My hope is that this book calls attention to wonderful things
about the Christian desert tradition that provided a foundation
for developments in contemplative prayer and ascetic practice
that have been legitimately transformational for Christians
throughout the centuries. I hope also that the book offers the
corrective we need in order to appreciate the complexity of
human experience, women's and men's, contained in the
Christian desert tradition. In light of contemporary crises of
all kinds—political, religious, cultural, social, and ecological—
there are fewer things more important than questioning our
assumptions about human experience in relation to God, each

---

30. *The Sayings of the Desert Fathers,* trans. Ward, 164.

other, ourselves, and the natural world. Tracing contemporary expectations of ourselves back to assumptions formed in late antiquity will allow us to consider different trajectories that might have been possible. Who knows what might come of rethinking women's experiences in these early Christian centuries? Who knows what ideas that stories of these women's lives might provide for articulating anew our own experience and for identifying what is really of value to us?

CHAPTER ONE

Making Space for Women Readers of the Christian Desert Tradition

Though few know much about the desert daughters and sons, the literature of the Christian desert tradition is still read by some for its charming stories of women and men given over as entirely as possible to encounter with God. Often the literature has been read by those within Christian monastic communities. More recently it has been "discovered" by Protestant evangelical readers and activists who cite its influence in their own formation of intentional community life, alternative social economies, and contemplative spiritual practices.[1] Increasingly, the literature has been read with appreciation by modern people like me who wish they'd had a monastic vocation or an opportunity to live within an intentional community such as a Catholic Worker or Jesuit Volunteer Corps household, beyond the immediate family. Significantly, the appeal

---

1. See, for instance, Jonathan Wilson-Hartgrove, *The Wisdom of Stability: Rooting Faith in a Mobile Culture* (Brewster, MA: Paraclete, 2010); Ian Mobsby and Mark Berry, *A New Monastic Handbook: From Vision to Practice* (Norwich: Canterbury, 2014); and Rory McEntee and Adam Bucko, *New Monasticism: An Interspiritual Manifesto for Contemplative Living* (Maryknoll, NY: Orbis Books, 2015).

of this literature comes at a time when many in contexts like North America feel isolated geographically and ideologically from family members and the community in which they were brought up. People like me read from outside cloister walls and are particularly drawn to this early tradition properly identified as *proto*monastic rather than monastic, because its inhabitants lived outside monastery walls, prior to the formalization of a certain kind of consecrated religious life that remains to our day. These individuals and the tales of their lives are often more accessible to modern readers than stories involving monks and nuns of later centuries with whom many readers do not share a religious vocation with its commitment to celibacy, obedience to community leadership and a rule, and the stability of life that monastic environments make possible and require for continuance.

The literature of the Christian desert tradition emerged from stories of men and women who were the revolutionaries of their day, countercultural exemplars who formed their own idiorhythmic rules of life and responded to and interacted with their own chosen spiritual companions. Thus, they offer contemporary readers a portrait of a lifestyle that, because independent of the explicit vocation that eventually derived from this context, might still feel possible for spiritual seekers today. From dwelling fruitfully in solitude to praying while one worked, from judiciously moderating one's experience of food or sleep or relationships to attending deeply to injurious habits of thought, the desert Christians' experiences contain a wealth of insight on the human condition and the seeking after and experiencing of the divine that remains as useful for those of us who remain outside monastery walls as it has been for centuries for those within such communities.

But just as there is much to cherish in the desert tradition, there is much as well that remains grievous, and even particularly offensive, to women. Just a cursory glance at a few pages of the sayings collections and the constant introductory repetition of "He also said. . . . He also said. . . . He also said. . . ." may set some women's teeth on edge. This kind of stitching of the sayings together may seem benign, but it indicates a reverence for men's words and a continual pointer to the men who uttered the words that may make some women want to close the book. That this chapter attempts to make space for the female reader means that we acknowledge these aspects of an androcentric text and move past them as signposts providing a clear view of the bias expressed in this text that virtually compels us to let other voices speak.

I remember a conversation with a colleague a few years back, also a scholar of the Christian desert tradition, who referred to a certain desert elder named Arsenius as "a grumpy old man." Arsenius is, in some respects, the exemplar solitary of the desert tradition, a figure whose desert solitude contrasted greatly with his former involvement with those living the high life in such cosmopolitan cities as Alexandria. Stories about Arsenius went on to influence the seventh-century ascetic, Isaac the Syrian, and his own privileged expression of Christian life as solitary. Hearing this colleague's characterization of Arsenius, I was at first shocked, then intrigued, and finally amused as I realized my own assumptions were being tested and revealed. Finally, I asked myself: Could Arsenius *really have been* a grumpy old man?[2] He certainly valued his peaceful solitary retreat to such an extent that he was rather rude to visitors (Arsenius 28) and even rated poorly his fellow desert dwellers who could discern the sound of reeds blowing in the wind while trying to pray (Arsenius 25), two representations of his personality that may not impress readers today. Similarly, might not "grumpy old men" be an apt appraisal of many of the figures whom we learn of and are expected to admire in the desert literature? Though it initially surprised,

---

2. Interestingly, this kind of question is explored by Chris L. de Wet in the article, "Grumpy Old Men?: Gender, Gerontology, and the Geriatrics of Soul in John Chrysostom," *Journal of Early Christian Studies* 24, no. 4 (2016): 491–521.

and even slightly pained, me to consider this possibility, this colleague's identification of Arsenius did much to awake me to the invitation to look more closely at the sayings collections and to consider how many of their heroes might have been "grumpy old men" and legitimately so. Many of them were dealing with internal contradictions between ideals and reality that would have made anyone grumpy. For instance, while the ability to be "alone with the Alone" was held up as an ideal virtue to develop, a saying such as Theonas's expresses a Christian countertext to this ideal (drawn perhaps from Matt 18:20): "Even if [one] acquires a virtue, God does not grant [that one] grace for [that person] alone" (Poemen 151). One needs the neighbor to share with, and with whom to experience God.

However, I have not only learned to look more closely beyond the representations of holy men in the sayings collections to their "real," and perhaps gritty, lives. I have also begun to peer into the margins of the stories, to recognize and greet characters who appear and say nothing or very little, to note their ephemeral passing, and to puzzle over why they appear, what kept them silent, and what they might have said had the storytellers remembered their words. This peering into the margins has, for me, yielded a new source of wisdom in the sayings.

Though the desert literature is so heterogeneous a collection, made up of anecdotes, teachings, lives, and histories, one of its common threads is its focus on exemplary men and their ordeals and successes. Sprinkled here and there, however, is the presence of a woman. Though three are named as known desert elders and have sayings attributed to them in the Alphabetical Collection of the desert sayings—Syncletica, Sarah, and Theodora—these women are exceptions. Others appear silently, seeming merely to occasion a moment of insight for men. These women were, nevertheless, leading their own lives, dealing with their own ordeals and successes, which seem not to have interested men. This book is an attempt to honor those lives, proposing avenues of thought to consider what these women's lives might have looked like. Such an attempt is motivated by my profound love for these stories and a desire that they be rehabilitated for contemporary and future readers. Reading past some of the bias related primarily to gender (but also to ethnicity and social status) that is expressed in the desert stories may allow some readers to access more readily the value that still remains a part of the Christian desert tradition, and even to discern and imagine new values for this tradition.

Non-Judgment or Judgment?

In this chapter, I explore assumptions around the traditional interpretations of stories contained in the sayings collections. Even as these assumptions are revealed and clarified, however, I suggest also an approach to the desert sayings that allows their underrepresented characters to offer something of value to the interpreter of this early Christian tradition—something that has, to date, been neglected. It is not surprising that these underrepresented characters are, principally, female. An example of such a story and such an approach may be useful here. This story appears in a chapter in the Systematic Collection called "against judging":

> Abba Poemen once came into the region of Egypt to dwell there, and there happened to be a brother living near him who had a wife. The elder was aware of this but did not ever condemn him. Now it happened that she gave birth one night, and, perceiving this, the elder called his junior brother, saying, "Take a measure of wine with you and give it to the neighbor, for today he is in need." His brothers were unaware of the matter, but he did as the elder told him to do. The brother [his neighbor] benefitted; he was conscience stricken, and, a few days later, he dismissed the woman (giving her whatever she needed). Then he came and said to the elder, "As of today I am repenting, Abba." He came and built himself a cell near the elder and often

went to him; the elder lighted him along the way of God
and gained possession of him. (Against Judging 20)

First, we may notice that this story represents what may seem
surprising to us: a situation that was still possible in the desert
before the institutionalization of monastic life—that is, this
early "monk" or single one (from the Greek *monachos*) had a
wife and child. Yet it also represents a desert Christian who
comes to see these relationships, entailing identities for himself
as husband and father, as problematic, given his life goals. We
see him conscience-stricken when dealt with gently, or *non-
judgmentally*, by his neighbor, Poemen, upon the delivery of
a child to the man's family. The story ostensibly has a happy
ending for the man, depriving himself of his wife and child,
so as to "repent" and live nearer to Poemen—indeed, in
slightly ominous language, to be taken "possession of" by
Poemen—and apparently to receive more teachings from him
about the kind of life men wanted to establish in the desert,
without women and without children.

Surprisingly, Lucien Regnault cites this story as proof that
the there was "no contempt of women among the desert
fathers."[3] In order to do so, however, Regnault has had to
abbreviate the story, showing only the parts of the story—the
giving of wine in celebration of the baby's birth—that are
proof of the "goodness with which the Desert Fathers treated
women who misbehaved with a monk."[4] Having read the story
in full, I hope we can see how the woman in this story has *not*
misbehaved with a monk; rather, we see more accurately the
man misbehaving *after* and prompted to do so by the giving
of Poemen's gift.

3. Lucien Regnault, *The Day-to-Day Life of the Desert Fathers*, trans.
Étienne Poirier Jr. (Petersham, MA: St. Bede's Publications, 1998), 30.
4. Ibid., 31.

Of what exactly is the man repenting as he leaves his family and joins Poemen's retinue? Given the morality of the Christian communities of this time and even of future times, he was not sinning by being with a wife and having a child with her. He was, however, living in a way that was *to become* incompatible with monastic reality and thus is represented after the fact as duplicitous in the desert context, as he appears to be one who has renounced sexual activity, to *be* monachos, when in fact he is not. An alternative morality was being developed in the desert context—by men—and this story documents its emergence: a seemingly more strenuous way of life, stripped both of familial responsibilities and pleasures, facilitated progress "along the way of God." We might appreciate that the man sent the woman and child away with everything they needed (shades of Abraham, Hagar, and Ishmael? cf. Gen 21:14), but still consider: Was this man acting aright? Is this really exemplary behavior and thus imitable behavior?

The inclusion of this story in the chapter on non-judgment affirms Poemen's activity as the exemplary, imitable one. He does not judge this man for having a wife and child, and neither should we. Poemen responds to the man's needs without broadcasting his situation; if we are as well-versed in Scripture as the desert Christians themselves, we probably hear echoes of 1 Peter 4:8 in Poemen's act of love that covers over a multitude of sins. But the premise of the man's actions being sin remains fundamentally in error. The partnered man acts upon Poemen's gesture of generosity as if it *were* judgment—he can somehow read the shaming implicit between the lines of Poemen's lack of shaming, in a paradoxical manner worthy of the sayings genre in general (there is almost always more in these stories than meets the eye)—and replaces his familial relations with that of a man capable of non-judgment, further affirming for us by this recognition of exemplarity what we, the readers, are to consider exemplary. Ironically, reading this story in the contemporary context evokes just this response from me: one of judgment.

My judgment is this: This man was not wrong for having had a wife and child. But this man was wrong in having sent away the woman and child with whom he had been making a home. What grounds this judgment? Two reasons: First, the social implications for this woman and child were injurious. We can sense the uneasiness of the tellers of this story around this aspect of the story in their inclusion of the detail that the man provided the woman with what she needed.[5] In this sense, the man imitates Poemen's gesture of gift-giving and provision in a way that cements their common identity as desert sons. However, clearly whatever this man could give his wife and new child would not be enough. What happened to her? Did she return to her family home? Did the child brought up without a father survive and even thrive? *Could* the two of them survive and thrive in the patriarchal culture of their time? We know from other desert sayings that women and children were dependent on men's work, income, and inheritance, so that in another desert saying we learn that it requires supernatural intervention from a desert elder named Milesius to converse with a dead man about how his death had come about (over the theft of money) and how to locate the stolen funds for his family's needs (Milesius 1). So that in yet another story we learn, similarly, that it takes Macarius's intervention on behalf of a weeping widow whose family, left destitute at her husband's death, is about to be enslaved to converse like Milesius with the dead man to find out where deposited funds have been stored (Macarius 7). It should not surprise us that women and children were so dependent on men but it should surprise us, and even cause us discomfort, that the woman and child in the story about Poemen's non-judgment, are offered as collateral damage in a man's spiritual quest. Indeed, that the women in the stories of Milesius and Macarius

---

5. Perhaps, too, we can sense Regnault's uneasiness in his interpretation of the desert men's charity in omitting recognition of the troubling aspects of this story.

appeal to desert sons for help suggests a terrible power these men of the desert accrued as they, themselves, as in the case of Poemen, occasioned the removal of male members of the family who would have helped the families survive and thrive.

This leads to the second reason why the man should not have sent away his wife and child: the spiritual implications were injurious, as well. Not just for the man, but for the emerging tradition and subsequent ideas of Christian discipleship that affirm this kind of action. The man had begun a life with this woman, and discarding her and their offspring at this point should be seen as insupportable of, rather than facilitating, spiritual life. That the man's actions are not represented that way in this story should register as problematic to us, and it should bring us to renewed consciousness and appreciation of what we do consider supportive of spiritual life.

While sudden ruptures to one's way of life are often seen as consistent with an experience of "conversion," such sudden ruptures affect others besides oneself. My point is that dedication to one's own spiritual formation at the cost of others' well-being should be discreditable, and we have to attend to these desert stories and what they say and what they don't say in order to bring these discreditable aspects of the stories and the subsequent tradition they helped form to further light. Indeed, to do so requires that we enter into a kind of judgment upon these stories, sympathetic to the many actors in the stories with whom we might share a desire to become more spiritually mature, more aware of the divine presence in our own lives and the lives we share with others. But we must also be critically reflective when it comes to noting the ways in which these desert sons and daughters acted upon that desire. Sometimes they may have been right. Sometimes they may have been wrong. In identifying these distinctions, we come to recognize to what degree we share some habits of thought in relation to the spiritual life we understand to be unfolding within and among us today.

Where Lies Wisdom?

The desert Christians learned wisdom from one another. They also learned wisdom from "outsiders" to the tradition, or those not obviously offering a spiritual teaching, though interpreted as doing so. This kind of learning and transformation constitutes a desert strategy of spiritual maturation and a pattern that we will duplicate in our reading and making sense of the peripheral women in the stories. Indeed, this kind of learning models for the contemporary reader how to look beyond the seemingly obvious to recognize and "read" wisdom in everyday situations. The desert sons and daughters themselves perform this "reading" strategy when, for instance, an elder observed that a dog was better than he for the dog loves and does not judge, both of which actions—loving and refraining from judgment—he ostensibly failed to perform (Anon 434). In this case, he learned from attentively observing the behavior of a dog, using the observation to identify his own values and condemn his failure to live up to them. Another saying tells of Poemen's deferring to a secular visitor rather than offer wisdom himself. He asks this devout visitor, a seller of vegetables who even admits to "buying cheap and selling dear," (Poemen 109) to offer the men assembled at Poemen's cell a wise saying. The fact that the visitor admits deficiency in Scriptural exegesis opens up another avenue for the communication of wisdom: story. Instead of offering the requested interpretation of Scripture, this visitor offers a parable that tells of "friends" who accompany one on the way to "see the Emperor" (that is, God). One friend goes half the journey; another goes as far as the imperial palace; another goes all the way inside to enter conversation with the one journeying and the Emperor. The men ask the visitor to explain his story and he does by identifying each friend sequentially as asceticism, chastity, and almsgiving. Not surprisingly does this story create a hierarchy of values, though maybe we can be surprised by his elevation of almsgiving when he has already admitted to dubiously-acquired success in business. Nevertheless, the story's wisdom is from an unlikely source and is communicated via an unlikely means.

Others learned from women not designated spiritual teachers and yet capable of communicating through their actions a truth that observers might apply to themselves. Pambo, for instance, observed an Alexandrian actress and was moved to understand something about himself he had not realized before: that he did not put as much effort into pleasing God as this woman apparently did to please her audience (Sorrow for Sin 32). Similarly, two other sayings recount Poemen's taking an occasion to observe a grieving woman sitting near where a beloved one had been buried to comment that the desert Christians, too, should be like that: grieving for their sins (Sorrow for Sin 24 and 25). Another saying, reported at secondhand, tells of a friend who observed Poemen in ecstasy and asked him about his experience; Poemen told how he had "been with" Mary at the side of the cross weeping. Poemen then expressed the wish that he, too, might always weep like that (Poemen 144). Seeing these sayings together invites me to wonder whether some level of theological abstraction occurred to offer a lesson from Poemen about the moral significance of Mary in the gospel, offering a lesson to Poemen, then to his friend Isaac, then to Joseph who told of the story, then to us. The other sayings remain rooted in the mundane world, reading the experience of real-life women to express a truth of the human condition, and an ordinary strategy of attentiveness and discernment concerning the everyday activities in one's life, rather than isolating wisdom to experiences within ecstatic states.

However, this truth concerning one's need to sorrow over sin remains ambiguous when "sin" is repeatedly associated with one's tempting thoughts and the desire to give in to them. Deliberately, the desert Christians spoke of conscious engagement with one's tempting thoughts as sinful, not having the tempting thought itself. If only these desert sons like

Poemen had been speaking of the sin of patriarchy, that would cause a woman to understand herself as so bereaved in losing a male loved one for reasons beyond the obvious love she may have felt for him! Cast adrift into a society that had never valued her womanhood, loss of association with and protection from a man was a situation for which men *should* share grief. Indeed, Sorrow for Sin 25 elaborates in full the reason for this woman's despair in a patriarchal world by stating that not only has she lost a husband but a son and brother. It is important that "father" is not included in the list of relationships that define this woman's identity. If it had been, an occasion would be lost for reinforcing the image of a patriarchal God, upon whom this woman—and all people—must depend.[6] Indeed, it is important that Poemen recommends that men acquire compunction such as this in order to live into the kind of life they were forming in the desert (the "monastic" life). Sorrow over the sin of patriarchy must be embraced by women and men alike. Not only does such sin influence the lives of women made vulnerable without the protection of male family members and friends, but such sin also impacts the men who continue to perpetuate it by requiring that they flourish at the expense of others—to understand their flourishing exists at the expense of others. This reality of human experience constitutes something to be not only sorrowed over but repented of, as well. We might also understand the theme of compunction (*penthos*) to include remorse over men's sinful dehumanizing behavior toward women and others. In the cases

---

6. Indeed, a desert son rebukes a messenger who comes to inform him of his father's death by claiming his "father" (i.e., God) is immortal. The text can be seen to use this anecdote to affirm the desert son's orthodoxy but also to redirect, painfully, attention from the biological to the spiritual in a more extreme way (that is, to God) rather than is more often done in redirecting affiliation to the desert elder himself (Advancing to Perfection 5).

mentioned here, though, each observation allowed the observer to reflect more closely upon and identify themselves by contrasting themselves with an "other"—whether animal or female. In a way then these unassuming figures took up the role of spiritual mentor, usually designated by *father* (abba) or *mother* (amma) as the recognized wisdom figure able to communicate by direct teachings and advice, as well as through their observed virtuous actions, how the desert disciple might become more spiritually mature.

Another, rather humorous, story tells of a young Macarius beset by *acedia*—relentless boredom—who ventures into the desert to relieve his boredom by seeking the help of whomever he first meets. Rather than the wise elder he might have hoped and expected to meet, he runs into a young boy herding oxen. Faithful to his resolution, Macarius requests wisdom of this boy, both admitting his situation of boredom and speaking of being hungry. Whether this hunger is literal or metaphorical is unclear, but when Macarius asks the boy what he should do, the boy takes him at his word and sensibly suggests that Macarius should eat. Macarius says he has already done so and remains hungry. The boy, again sensibly, suggests that he eat again. Macarius explains he has eaten many times and always remained hungry, to which the boy says: "Perhaps you are an ass, abba, because you want to be always munching." The story, told in the first person, relates that Macarius went his way, edified, having received a significant spiritual teaching (Anon 490). Certainly this story is really about desire more generally, and the anxiety that desert Christians experienced as they understood themselves to be desiring creatures, whose needs—once met—merely recurred. Distinguishing legitimate needs from illegitimate was, of course, the project of the spiritual life, and yet the "hunger" of Macarius's experience leads to some humor and wisdom on the part of the boy's plain-speaking. The story is also about identity: Who is Macarius really? Is he the person he wants to be, while desire (to eat) persists? Having been identified as an "ass" by someone as unlikely as a young ox-herder, is he willing to reconsider his hunger?

Seeking and finding "wisdom" in unexpected places is already a process set in motion within the desert sayings in stories such as these. In this book, I seek to extend our vision to include those figures, often women, in the margins of the text—from whom the men in the text *might have* learned wisdom, and often did not. When thinking again about the man who sent his wife and child away, we might look for how the woman and her actions could be considered a source of wisdom just as important to us as Poemen's generosity toward the new family and restraint in judging the father of the new child. Though the story—not surprisingly—directly quotes both Poemen and the repentant man and yet renders the woman speechless, the woman speaks in giving birth, speaking aloud in doing so her husband's relations with her that he later finds problematic enough to disown her and the child as evidence of the relationship. She speechlessly vanishes, offering no retaliatory threats for the man's disturbance of the social order in which men making a home with a wife and children do not send them away. She makes no claims on him, suggesting she may have had low status with regard to her class, as well as her gender. A wealthy woman or a woman with a powerful enough family to back her might have insisted on her rights as a mother to the man's child. The restraint modeled by the woman must have been just what many of the men in the Christian desert wished the women they knew—mothers, sisters, friends, visitors—to adopt. But her action of birth-giving remains to speak truth and remind us that some of the uneasiness appearing in the sayings collections around women might have had something to do with men's desire to avoid facing, and to even silence, a disturbing truth: that of their own identity as men created to be in relationship with women, as well as men.

Peripheral Women

Who *were* these underrepresented figures of the Christian desert tradition on whom I want to focus our attention? Some of the women among them have been aptly characterized as "forgotten," as "virgins of God," as "female men of God," and as harlots.[7] While these characterizations are useful to varying degrees, this book also proposes that many contemporary female readers of the Christian desert tradition are likely to notice that the literature is populated by figures who do not fit the stereotype of the late antique ascetic female who, above all, strove to emulate or even surpass the late antique ascetic male. Indeed, many of the women I would like to draw attention to in this book, such as the wife and mother mentioned above, do not fit such a stereotype *at all*. Of the four characterizations offered above, "forgotten" is the only one that certainly applies to the woman referred to above who gave birth to a child in the desert and who was deserted by her husband. "Forgotten" is a category that will apply to most of the women whose lives I point to in this book. They were not necessarily reformed fallen women upheld in the tradition for their unusual life turnaround when devoting themselves to God. They were not necessarily "manly" women whose virtue was akin to or exceeded what men could manage in their own spiritual lives. They were not virgins, metaphorically or literally.

The women who did fit these categories, and more accurately contributed to creating these categories, of the stereotypical

---

7. See, respectively: Laura Swan, *The Forgotten Desert Mothers: Sayings, Lives, and Stories of Early Christian Women* (Mahwah, NJ: Paulist Press, 2001); Susanna Elm, *'Virgins of God': The Making of Asceticism in Late Antiquity* (Oxford: Oxford University Press, 1994); Gillian Cloke, *'This Female Man of God': Women and Spiritual Power in the Patristic Age, AD 350–450* (New York, NY: Routledge, 1995); Benedicta Ward, *Harlots of the Desert: A Study of Repentance in Early Monastic Sources*, CS 106 (Kalamazoo, MI: Cistercian Publications, 1987).

late antique ascetic female were often known as revered desert mothers or *ammas*. They taught other women and men out of their deep experiential engagement with God, Scripture, their own deepest desires and fallibilities, and the natural world around them. Much of this deep experiential engagement was facilitated by strategies of deprivation, commonly referred to as renunciation or asceticism, as these desert women used their wisdom to discern what held them back from fully engaging God, Scripture, their deepest selves, and the natural world. They then used their wisdom to undertake practices that would further disengage them from those barriers and thus become more available to experiential engagement with the (O)ther.

There were other women, though, who appear in the sayings and stories of the desert tradition as mothers, sisters, daughters, wives, friends, and visitors whose roles in the stories were decidedly peripheral. We have already been introduced to one of them who was disowned by her partner and told to evacuate the home they had shared. Another such story and my following commentary will further introduce us to the status of "peripheral" I focus on in this book and to what is revealed about the desert dynamic by focusing on the peripheral. A desert elder related of himself the following story:

> Once when I was staying at Oxyrrynchos with a priest who was a great giver of alms, a widow came asking him for a little grain. "Go, get a cloth [bag], and I will measure it out to you," he said to her. When she brought it, he felt the cloth with his hand, saying, "This is a big one!" – which put the widow to shame. When the widow had left, I said to him, "Did you sell the grain to the widow, Abba?" "No," he said; "I gave her charity." Then I said, "So, if you have given it to her entirely as charity, why did you quibble so minutely and put her shame?" (Hospitality 16)

The story's central focus is two men in conversation, reflecting on an action performed by one of the men while interacting with a woman. The moral adduced between the two is that one should not "quibble over insignificant things." Indeed, the anecdote is offered by a desert elder to illustrate the general observation with which the saying opens: "There can be a person frequently employed in many good works whom the evil one causes to quibble over insignificant things in order to make him lose the reward for all the good things he achieves" (ibid.). This story from the man's past serves to illustrate his point, and we can glean and even extend the bit of wisdom intended for us from this exchange: that one should not only quibble with others over insignificant things, but one should be courteous, kind, and hospitable when giving charity, as opposed to giving begrudgingly. If we fail to be courteous, kind, and hospitable, we lose whatever merit our virtuous actions are thought to accrue for us. This is the *central* point of the story, certainly occasioned by the presence and need of the woman to which the men respond but clarified by the discourse of men, both as the male characters interact in the story itself and the male narrator later tells the story ostensibly to other men. Shifting our focus to the peripheral, we attend to the woman herself. What wisdom, what "way of love" do her actions reveal?

To begin, we note the storyteller reveals the woman asked for a "little" grain. Though her speech is not recorded in the saying, we hear her indirectly. (The men's voices, of course, are recorded verbatim, allowing us to understand where the men's attention focused and what they and those who retold their story remembered and found important.) Expectations are immediately set up between the woman and man with the woman's request that makes her return with a large bag surprising the generous priest. Is this a demonstration of greed? Or did the woman have prescient knowledge of the priest's generosity so that her initial request was a humble or even perhaps shrewd testing of the waters? The confidence she shows in returning with a large bag is indeed poignant. We know she is a widow. She has no husband and perhaps no sons to help her support a family, if she has one. She displays an ability to discern the priest's generosity as a given, and refrains from speaking back when he makes an offhand comment about the size of her bag. Culturally, such a talking back might have been impossible for her, in any case, defenseless and at the man's mercy as she was. However, her silence is also the kind of thing about the story that enables contemporary readers to engage imagination and plumb this interaction for wisdom applicable to our own (men and women's) situation.

A piece of this wisdom might entail considering how the woman recognized a discrepancy between the man's actions and his words, that his heart was in the right place despite the slip he made in words to reveal some kind of anxiety about the giving away of the grain she had asked for. Would such generosity compromise his ability to help others? Or, even more aptly, did he feel some kind of embarrassment about his own access to goods, in being able to fill the woman's large bag, to benefit, we might put it today, from a patriarchal system designed not only to benefit men in the first place but then to preserve their privilege through giving them access to and control over distributing essential goods? Could the woman's reticence indicate recognition of this troubled aspect of men's experience, and a loving invitation to learn for himself what was at the source of his irritation with her? Rather than imposing on him her own interpretation of his action (as his male guest, the narrator of the story, did), the woman operates as an open space in the story—as expansive as her bag—to indicate the dimensions of men's lives that might yet be filled.

Moreover, what might be said further of this male friend who observed the exchange? Did his presence have anything to do with prompting the priest's remark? As these men are the only speakers in the story, we can imagine their intercourse as not only verbal but ideological as one observes and critiques the other's actions. A comment the priest might have made to the woman, if he and she were alone, may have been quite different from a comment he felt expected to make, either for the woman's benefit or, more accurately perhaps, for the observing man's benefit—to show him that the priest remains in control of the situation. To reinforce the male privilege that he and his friend share, he is obliged in some respects to put down the woman as grasping for more than might seem her due, and in some way thus threatening.

In short, there are a variety of options for considering what prompted the man's words, and for responding as the woman in the story responded—with silence. She is apparently meant to be shamed, and yet are we convinced of her shame? We have only the storyteller's word for it to confirm this claim. He supplies no clues from the woman's demeanor to confirm this claim, unless her seemingly utter lack of presence (merely because speechless) in the story is meant to confirm her inconsequential status in the context of men exchanging words about her . . . or rather about a man's actions in response to her presence manifested as need a man could supply.

We might think then of the woman as needy, but also as confident that she would not be turned away with her big bag. She may be understood as courageous and hardy, as not willing to let a man's assessment of her actions prevent her acquisition of needed sustenance for her and a family for which she may have needed to provide. In this story, perhaps we hear resonance with the persistence of the Canaanite woman who does not let Jesus's observation about the inappropriateness of her request for healing deter her from getting what she, and her daughter, needed (Mark 7:24-30; Matt 15:21-28). Indeed, the desert story is more efficient in conveying its female character's confidence, through the simple act of showing up with a bigger bag than was expected, than in the detailed verbal exchange between Jesus and the Canaanite woman. Nevertheless, both women were satisfied. That the means of satisfaction were provided through a man might prove problematic to female readers of the desert sayings collections. However, the woman's wisdom in understanding, applying to, and receiving from the source of nourishment available to her given her limited circumstances remains instructive to readers today.

Further, I take this story to indicate how the female reader of the sayings might approach the Christian desert tradition in general—with a "large bag," confident to receive from it some sustenance for spiritual growth, even if it appears to be given begrudgingly. If, in some way, such a reader feels that careless speech is meant to shame her—as indeed, she will feel, if she reads at all attentively—we could, in turn, use the opportunity to cultivate compassion for the speaker's situation and what the speech could indicate about that situation: anxiety over resources to be distributed to all, anxiety toward the brazen quality of approach that suggests and even asserts that there is more to be given than what the giver thought they had power or liberty to give, and anxiety over collaborating in a socio-religious system designed to continue to marginalize certain of its members. As we may know from our own personal experience, the diffusing of one's own shame is often facilitated by attempts to shame another.

Countering Assumptions

As a key hermeneutical move for examination of women's experience in history is attending to voices "offstage,"[8] this book makes audible those women on the periphery, who often seem to persist in the tradition merely to provide a compelling "other" to the centralized male figures—and even to female figures who best duplicated the masculine ideal. I have just offered a couple portraits of such peripheral figures in the woman partnered to a desert disciple who bore a child with him and in the widowed woman appealing to a priest for grain.

8. Majella Franzmann, *Women and Religion* (New York, NY: Oxford University Press, 2000), 67–103.

Women such as these also persist, however, with a message of their own and elaborating a culture of their own. These women and their conversation and company and acts of caring inhabit the desert sayings and stories in important ways, and they invite us to listen to and learn from them just as much as from the (usually male) ascetics ostensibly in the foreground. These are women who, despite their experiences of anger, fear, loss, sadness, and certainly of being silenced, nevertheless convey an ethic which we might best characterize as love. They remain persistently in the stories, creating a space of non-assimilation and resistance to the emerging monastic paradigm (inclusive of both men and women), and remind us of other modes of Christian discipleship beyond that espoused by the normalizing activity of renunciation.

In part, I want in this book to check the tendency in the Christian spiritual tradition to identify its key representatives of holiness or wholeness within the monastic experience; scholars have already begun to recognize the importance of marginalized lay individuals within the medieval, reformation, counterreformation, and contemporary periods and to locate an important spirituality in non-monastic, non-clerical lifestyles—to affirm how so-called "ordinary" individuals could have compelling experiences of God and their own devotional practices just as exemplary and transformative as those found amongst consecrated religious. It is important to point out that this recognition within the history of Christian spirituality is recent, and there is a reason for its recent development: increasingly those employed in scholarly pursuits in theology and its various sub-disciplines, such as biblical studies, ethics, and spirituality, are no longer those professedly religious—whether clerics or monastics or the like. Thus, their own identification outside the vocationally religious has invited scholars, such as myself as a married, lay Catholic, to discern sources of wisdom and holiness or wholeness outside parameters typically reserved within the cloister and even within the Christian churches. This is an important development in the history of the scholarship of Christian spirituality, and one that has deeply self-implicating components. In other words, if the study of Christian spirituality is self-implicating—that is, it occurs within the pursuit of wisdom for the researcher[9]—then the religious status of contemporary scholars has much to do with determining the subjects studied. Similarly, if in the past fifty years women have begun to enter theological discourse as scholars and pastoral ministers alongside men, they also have shifted the focus of such discourse about Christian tradition to include more women's voices and experiences.

The same shift of focus that scholars of the medieval period have effected is important within the late antique period, when much interpretation of the emerging lay movement focuses on its protomonastic qualities. Instead of allowing the spirituality of this movement, available to us still in the desert sayings, lives, and histories, to default to being representative of early monastic experience, what would happen if we focused on how desert spirituality functions as representative of a broader, countercultural movement,[10] explicitly in continuity with forms of life found in the New Testament, open to all Christians and even *expected* of all Christians? How would this allow the desert tradition to still speak to all forms of Christian life as simply *how life should be lived* and not as representative of a specific emerging monastic tradition, offering ideas about

---

9. See Sandra M. Schneiders, "A Hermeneutical Approach to the Study of Christian Spirituality," in *Minding the Spirit: The Study of Christian Spirituality*, ed. Elizabeth A. Dreyer and Mark S. Burrows (Baltimore, MD: Johns Hopkins University Press, 2005), 58–59. Also, Philip Sheldrake, "Spirituality and Its Critical Methodology," in *Exploring Christian Spirituality: Essays in Honor of Sandra M. Schneiders, IHM*, ed. Bruce H. Lescher and Elizabeth Liebert (Mahwah, NJ: Paulist Press, 2006), 22–24.

10. Belden C. Lane has been an important voice articulating this "countercultural" stance within recent scholarship. See, for instance, his "Desert Attentiveness, Desert Indifference: Countercultural Spirituality in the Desert Fathers and Mothers," *CrossCurrents* 44, no. 2 (1994): 193–206.

ascetic and contemplative practice that would only be taken up and furthered by those in consecrated religious life? My hunch is that it has been convenient for interpreters of the desert tradition to consider it protomonastic, as then the ideals it represents as to how life should be lived leave an "ordinary" Christian off the hook, so to speak. Ascetic values, in particular, might then be legitimately abandoned wholesale instead of adopted with discernment to rebalance lives that are, in our modern context, increasingly out of balance.

In continuity with questioning the impulse to make this movement and its literature protomonastic, intended for those called to consecrated religious life, several assumptions must be described and proposals offered to undermine such assumptions. To make space for contemporary readers of the Christian desert tradition to notice, reflect on, and respond to the lives of underrepresented figures in the literature, we must address at least three assumptions about the body of literature making up this tradition that have constrained interpretation of these sayings and stories. By acknowledging the implications of these assumptions, we begin to move beyond the interpretations of the literature within which these assumptions, and the living communities who formed and continue to uphold them, constrain their readers. These assumptions have to do with the readership of the Christian desert tradition, the relationship between master and disciple, and the word of wisdom exchanged between men as the primary locus of spiritual value.

- *Assumption #1: Because monastic communities were primarily responsible for the preservation of the desert literature, all of its main figures and teachings find their relevance within the monastic paradigm.*

As mentioned before, to see the literature of the Christian desert tradition as exclusively protomonastic and indicative of future monastic ideals is to miss a great deal of value in the

sayings and to risk dismissing much of what is in them as pro-
motional of the monastic life solely. While it is true that many
characters in the desert tradition espoused ascetic lifestyles
which eventually became a central feature of monastic life, many
characters did not. Even when they did, they did so as part of
their Christian, not as part of their protomonastic, identity.

Perhaps it is useful here to point out as well that not all
modern monastic readers of this literature recognize it as descriptive or even prescriptive of their own monastic vocations.
Indeed, the respected Benedictine scholar of the desert tradition, Columba Stewart, helpfully explains the incongruence
between contemporary monastic readers and those to whom
the desert literature was/is ostensibly addressed. He cites four
ways that the desert tradition might strike its contemporary
readers, monastic or otherwise, with dissonance rather than
affinity: (1) the tradition's doctrinal polemic and tendency
toward orthodox triumphalism, (2) the tradition's ascetic
orientation, (3) the tradition's unspoken assumptions concerning gender and sexual normativity, and (4) the tradition's lack
of interest in the natural world.[11] While not all of these areas
of incongruence will disturb every reader, these aspects of the
tradition do raise important questions for contemporary readers who engage this literature and find value in it. Do we let
this literature validate our taking firm insider/outsider stances
when relating to those of other religious traditions? Do we let
its valorization of extreme forms of asceticism affect the way
we relate to people capable of/not capable of restraint? Do
we let its misogynist and homophobic expressions inform our
self-understanding and understanding of others, and legislate
our own relationships? And finally, do we let its demonizing
of the wilderness enable and justify our destruction of the
natural world? Each of these questions reminds us of the fal-

11. Columba Stewart, " 'We'?: Reflections on Affinity and Dissonance
in Reading Early Monastic Literature," *Spiritus* 1, no. 1 (2001): 98–100.

libility—and reality—of the desert tradition. As stylized as the stories appear in some cases, they still represent real people with real fallibilities. Just like any other person, sometimes they were right. Sometimes they were wrong.

This book proposes undermining the assumption of the literature's protomonastic quality through demonstrating important dimensions of Christian life that do not resemble or anticipate later monastic patterns. An example of this would be the partnered relationships we just witnessed in stories of women bearing children and women widowed as part of the human community of which the desert tradition speaks. All the while, we will endeavor, however, to preserve, as appropriate, ascetic ideals in the textual tradition as representative of the *Christian* life Jesus called his followers to in the gospels (Luke 9:23 and parallels).

- *Assumption #2: Spiritual formation, the cultivation of discernment, and communication about the vicissitudes of the spiritual life and transformation are best accomplished through the master-disciple relationship.*

Emphasis on master-disciple relations saturates the desert sayings and, indeed, accounts in part for the fact the sayings exist at all. The desert variation of this traditional pedagogical model of relationship draws on New Testament parallels and earlier philosophical models in the ancient world that explicate how truth is communicated and received. From the New Testament, we see Christ as represented as the ultimate Teacher, a revelation of the true God, whom his followers were urged to imitate (John 13). From earlier philosophical models, we see teaching and learning occurring as a process of recalling to memory what the disciple already knows. It likely goes without saying that these models were mostly male. Though apocryphal gospels give women such as Mary Magdalene authoritative status as having receiving *gnosis* or knowledge from Jesus to

pass on to other apostles, and women such as the fourth-century
Hypatia of Alexandria and Macrina the Cappadocian taught
within their own philosophical and familial circles, whether
pagan or religious, respectively, these women were certainly
exceptions. Most women remained outside learned circles, let
alone having access to roles that would give them authority over
men. Nevertheless, the biblical association of the Hebrew
hochmah and the Greek *sophia* with the female suggests that all
along in the Judeo-Christian traditions an elaboration of wisdom as women's domain could have been made.

Even if this relationship of master/disciple was normative
as the context in which teaching and learning took place, we
have already seen how learning opportunities could occur in
the most mundane of settings, such as the field in which oxen
were feeding or the home in which a gift from a neighbor was
received. This book thus proposes undermining the assumption that the master-disciple relationship is essential to spiritual
growth through demonstrating two things: (1) how key learning moments in the sayings occur outside this so-called paradigmatic relationship, for instance between Macarius and the
ox-herding boy, and (2) how reliance on this model cripples
the seeker from living into the fullness of his or her own
unique experiential understanding of God.

- *Assumption #3: The "word" received by a disciple from an
  elder is the privileged locus of wisdom and catalyst for transformative spiritual experience, and thus has universal significance for anybody (within a monastic community)
  desiring to mature spiritually.*

This assumption follows from the previous two, in that the
ongoing relevance of sayings contained in the desert tradition
literature seems to have "spoken to" or meant something significant to people who both heard these stories and read them,
with the "word" achieving a universal status—primarily for

those committed to monastic life—dislocated from its originating occasion, whatever we can know of this. Scholars of
the desert tradition recognize the problematic nature of uni-
versalizing wisdom in this manner,[12] and such recognition has
prompted a need to recognize that the sayings originally address a specific person's needs and a specific person's understanding (faulty or perceptive) of that person's needs. That
we forget this quality of the sayings causes us to be reductive
of both the person who addressed the "word" and the one to
whom it was addressed—both of whom were unique individuals, quite unlike the representative "types" that begin to
emerge in the sayings collections. In addition, this assumption
locates the ongoing spiritual relevance of the desert sayings
in words exchanged primarily by men. This book proposes
undermining the assumption that a "word" exchanged between people constitutes the privileged source of wisdom
through demonstrating that the wisdom of the Christian desert tradition can also appear in anecdotes—storied experience—and in embodied expressions of love just as in explicit
teachings, in the widow's reluctance to either accept the shame
laid on her by the priest who spoke disparagingly of her big
bag or retaliate in word or action for a failure in the man's
wholehearted generosity. Further, while drawing conclusions
from these stories that offer wisdom to contemporary readers

12. "Those who came to the elders seeking 'a word' did so not because
they wanted or needed an extended spiritual discourse. They sought instead
to have their very particular needs and concerns addressed by direct, immediate words of salvation, power, truth, assurance, and even tenderness." Douglas
Burton-Christie, *The Word in the Desert: Scripture and the Quest for Holiness
in Early Christian Monasticism* (New York: Oxford University Press, 1993),
134. Christie also quotes Thomas Merton here: "The answers were not intended to be general, universal prescriptions. Rather, they were originally
concrete and precise keys to particular doors that had to be entered, at a given
time, by given individuals." Merton, *The Wisdom of the Desert: Sayings of the
Desert Fathers of the Fourth Century* (Boston: Shambhala, 2004), 12.

of the sayings, we will also not assume that the same wisdom for all readers can be drawn from what we see in the sayings. A collective wisdom will be elaborated but not forced.

All three of these assumptions indicate that women readers of the desert sayings are invited to be resistant readers, to be readers able to recognize the operation of these assumptions and to look further into the stories to see beyond whatever serves to reinforce these assumptions. Certainly, contemporary readers cannot easily discard centuries of historical interpretation of the early Christian spiritual tradition; we cannot simply throw away how this tradition has nourished subsequent movements and contributed to positioning the global Christian community where it is today. However, we *can* attempt to recognize and savor the taste of clear water closer to its source, to use an image from Thomas Merton's *The Wisdom of the Desert*. In the opening to Merton's own collection of favorite sayings, he proposes an image of a brook and how the nearer to the source we are the purer the water will taste to us.[13] We, twenty-first-century readers, are inevitably downstream, and further downstream with each generation. Yet, if it has proved problematic to contemporary scholars to try to retrieve the pure water of original sources, we can at least attend to the fact that our drinking today *is* contaminated and begin to "filter out" the detritus of accumulated assumptions about the tradition over the centuries—three of which assumptions this chapter briefly surveys.

In addition to inviting contemporary readers to be resistant readers, I invite contemporary readers to be constructive readers, entering into compassionate dialogue with the wise women and men of the desert with imagination and creativity, willing to experiment with cultivating and exercising an empathetic sensibility that allows us to see beyond depictions of

---

13. Thomas Merton, "Author's Note," in *The Wisdom of the Desert*, viii.

desert daughters and desert sons in the sayings as *what was* to consideration of *what might have been*. The interpretive process I employ in this book thus requires us to not only draw onto center stage offstage voices, or into main roles those who have traditionally been assigned support roles. The process also requires that we supply "gaps" in the narratives with sufficient attention to register the significance that such gaps exist in the first place and to creatively account for what might have been excised when such gaps were created, intentionally or unintentionally. In doing so, we do not necessarily "speak for" the silenced women in the tradition, but we allow our notice of their silenced and their softened voices to extend the possibilities for understanding more about not only others but about ourselves in relation to God.

CHAPTER TWO

"A Woman's Body is Fire"

Anxious Interactions
in the Christian Desert

A person beginning to read the desert sayings organized thematically in the Systematic Collection would find a lot of good advice in the collection's first chapter, on the theme of "advancing toward perfection." Although feminist readers might be suspicious of a program of spiritual advancement with "perfection" as its goal, the advice in this chapter is not gender-specific. That is, though it uses masculine pronouns and features only exchanges between men, the chapter's contents need not be understood as voicing ethical and ascetic ideals addressed to or valued only by men. For instance, the first saying, attributed to Antony, teaches: "Always have God before your eyes wherever you go" (Advancing 1). Indeed, this instruction helps us open the sayings wider than we might otherwise open them: it not only addresses the desert hermit stationed in solitude in his cell but also, and even especially, the one who is "on the go." The saying presupposes a mobile listener who may have many other distractions "before their eyes" so as to warrant a reminder to keep God in that privileged place. Such a mobile listener might be the person tending a flock in a faraway field, the person weaving a mat by a river, the person engaged in selling wares in the Alexandrian marketplace, even the person washing clothes or tending a garden or caring for children. They are all enjoined to "always have God before [their] eyes." We, too, might easily take such a teaching to heart.

Other precepts in this opening chapter that any reader, regardless of gender, might find useful include not regretting past actions, telling the truth, loving others, and making a fresh start every day. The range of actions conducive to psychological health and social harmony that these desert Christians thought made them more available to God is broad, and it remains perennially relevant to the contemporary Christian and even, at times, the non-religious reader.

Equally important in this opening chapter on advancing toward perfection is the affirmation of the diversity of virtuous actions to which one might be called, and implicit in this affirmation is the refraining from considering oneself better than others because of an ability to do something others can't. Thus, Nisteros answers a question with a question when asked what particular good work a person should do, by saying, "Are not all undertakings equal?" He then justifies his response by citing biblical exemplars Abraham, Elijah, and David (all men, of course!), whose diverse "good works" of hospitality, maintaining silence, and humility, respectively, pleased God equally (Advancing 18). A later saying in the collection even appeals to the episcopal authority of Cyril, fifth-century bishop of Alexandria, who, in response to a similar question, endorses both the active and contemplative lives, associating them respectively with biblical exemplars Moses and Elijah (Discretion 178). Given such affirmation of diverse vocations, we might be surprised to find antagonism toward women and toward lifestyles that include women. Shouldn't women have been welcomed within the Christian desert tradition as having their own way of being with God, and others? Shouldn't men who had women in their lives have been welcomed within the Christian desert tradition as having their own way of being with God? Shouldn't the literature of the Christian desert tradition reflect this broad inclusivity? When it does so, it seems to do so grudgingly. The logical conclusion of teachings of the kind described in this paragraph would lead to inclusion of women in the desert environment and when the sayings exclude, or seem to exclude, them, we may feel justifiably annoyed, and yet compassionate toward the Christians of this time trying to puzzle out the radical implications of the gospel to which they were devoted.

Though women will appear as primary players in *this* book as we tease out evidence of their presence in the Christian desert and their contribution to the Christian desert tradition, relating to the gendered other was for most of these desert men exceedingly problematic. The extent to which their inclusion reached was limited to diverse masculine ways of being Christian. And even this reach could be seen as artificial, as value accrued to more heroic instances of superhuman living—those able to live alone, to do without food and water, without sleep, etc. The check on such value being associated with superhuman heroics indicated by the sayings on the value of diverse vocations mentioned above, reveals an uneasiness with the tendency to valorize particular actions; and, yet, this check was neither systematic nor thorough enough as it still posited an either/or among, increasingly celibate, men. A certain level of renunciation was a given among these desert sons; whether it expressed itself in a communal or solitary setting then became the only arena for distinctions the desert literature expresses uneasiness about.

Nevertheless, we may assume that when desert sayings are not gender-specific, men and women alike can use them profitably. However, there are plenty of sayings that do reveal their assumption that only a man is in pursuit of holiness. A reader thus who encounters the instruction "Maintain no friendship with a woman" in the first chapter of the Systematic Collection of desert sayings (Advancing 13) first senses the tradition's exclusionary status in addressing men and, more specifically, men who felt that friendships with women would compromise their own spiritual identity and obstruct their progress on the spiritual journey. And yet, that such a reminder was necessary indicates there were men who maintained friendships with women. A reader of such sayings might understandably be perplexed and even alienated when grappling with such advice and its implications. This particular saying about friendship is the only reference to women in the first chapter, as no women are recorded as having spoken a saying about "advancing toward perfection." That omission itself may be telling, in that women could be said to be more wary than men of sensibilities based on progressing toward and achieving so-called "perfection." Even more unsettling for female readers is the extended story in chapter two about a female visitor to Arsenius. This is the first story in the Systematic Collection in which a woman has physical presence, and she is—not surprisingly—rejected. Arsenius's treatment of her is not unusual, for him or for his companions, and could be said to symbolize, and even set the standard for, many of the desert sons' relationships to women.

This female visitor, who is apparently rich and—of course—unnamed in the story, travels from Rome to visit the revered elder of whom she has heard so much. Arsenius responds to her visit angrily, assuming the woman's visit is only for the purpose of returning to Rome with a kind of elevated status for having visited Arsenius—an assumption that certainly reveals Arsenius's excessive self-regard, something not shamed in the story as it might have been, given the high value of humility among the desert Christians. Indeed, the story's plot involves Arsenius's shaming the woman for presuming to visit him, and her subsequent acceptance of this shame and her repentance for having bothered him. That this shaming strategy echoes that between the priest and the widow seeking grain indicates the source of these men's anxiety: women asking something of men, something the men did not understand themselves able to give. In Arsenius's case, we also hear his expressing concern over the continued viability of his way of life, should the unnamed Roman visitor return to home and spread word of Arsenius. These women pose an existential and material threat, and the men's rebukes may be seen as arising from visceral cognition of that threat. In this case, the story ends: "she was healed in her mind; she went back home rejoicing" when convinced by Archbishop Theophilus—the intermediary between the two—that Arsenius's bark is worse than his bite (Hesychia 10). Clearly these stories are included in the sayings collections in order to school men in their relations with irritating female visitors, but also to school women to know better than to bother the men, indicating tangentially that these stories were not just collected for the sake of the later monastic communities but had value more broadly within the Christian communities. The bottom line of stories such as these was to safeguard the men's ways of life.

Certainly, stories like these pose problems for female readers who can hear the following assertions proffered through explicit instruction and, implicitly, through anecdote: (1) men are unable to spiritually mature when distracted by women, (2) women should know better than to bother men whose primary goal in life is to spiritually mature and, (3) when women do not act on such knowledge about their tempting identity it is legitimate for men to scold them. The problematic nature of these implications has been acknowledged by contemporary monastic interpreters of this tradition, Columba Stewart and Louis Leloir.[1]

---

1. Columba Stewart, "The Portrayal of Women in the Sayings and Stories of the Desert," *Vox Benedictina* 2, no. 1 (1985): 5–23. Louis Leloir, "Woman and the Desert Fathers," *Vox Benedictina* 3, no. 3 (1986): 207–27.

Men's wishful thinking was that the desert remain a place where no women might be found; this was, however, not true of the desert, though very few of the women who might have made a home in the desert appear in the literary record of the early Christian desert movement. When they do appear, they occasion anxiety, gynophobia, and even misogyny on the part of the men who dominate the discourse, in general, and the discourse about such women. These experiences of anxiety, gynophobia, and misogyny do not represent the whole tradition, by any means. But the fact that they remain central in the stories helps us uncover reasons for why there is such a scarcity of information about women's spiritual lives at this time.

Though the words "gynophobia" and "misogyny" are easily understandable within the discourse of Western culture, less common are words indicating fear or hatred of men. They exist as linguistic possibilities, but how often have we heard or used the words *androphobia* or *misandry*? Indeed, the title of a recent film (2017)—*The Misandrists*—is illuminating, in that its strangeness in everyday discourse reveals how seldom women's experience has been so named: Is it that women have *not* feared or hated men, or is it that they have not been permitted to express such feelings? It is not only that men have not permitted such words to become common lingo in the language, but that women who might have used such words have not been listened to enough—have not used these words either with one other or with men to exchange information about or express feelings of fear or hatred. Such absences in our discourse not only point out how infrequently women have voiced these experiences or been listened to as they voiced these experiences, but also how infrequently it has been thought important to record their having done so. In this chapter, we will make a journey through experience of men's anxiety, fear of and hatred toward women in the Christian desert, in order to continue to chip away at the notion that women were not a part or even an important part of the desert tradition.

Desert Anxiety

There were many things that Christians living in late antiquity might feel anxious about. Intermittent periods of religious intolerance and persecution, economic and political instability in the Roman Empire, robbery and violence one might experience while traveling, and a host of related concerns affected a person's everyday life, let alone their religious identity and practice.[2] For desert Christians, an additional anxiety arose. Many desert Christians had an opportunity to really scrutinize their participation in a corrupt social system, and as they did so, they realized they had an important opportunity to witness to an alternative way of life. How that might unfold, whether organically from their own adopted ways of life that "desert" (literal and metaphorical) made possible or from intentional witness to pilgrims, could be a source of anxiety. Indeed, for desert disciples eager to set up their own way of life in the desert, finding a physical place and support system wherein that could happen were additional material and psychological concerns prompting anxiety—and its remedy: absolute trust in God's provision. This understandable experience of anxiety prompted beneficial teachings—teachings, indeed, still useful to readers of this tradition who deal with their own anxieties. In this section, I address two areas of anxious concern for the desert ascetics: material and psycho-spiritual.

To begin with, material concern for the desert Christian's safety in remote areas of wilderness were well-founded. When one elder was asked: "Why am I afraid when I walk about in the desert?" and the elder answers, "Because you are still alive" (Sayings 5), we are able to take this exchange to indicate two things. Not only is there existential risk to dwelling in isolation

2. E. R. Dodds, *Pagan and Christian in an Age of Anxiety: Some Aspects of Religious Experience from Marcus Aurelius to Constantine* (Cambridge: Cambridge University Press, 1965).

and realizing the deepening relationship with God and one's own self that such isolation might make possible (or obstruct), there is also the physical danger of hyenas, lions, crocodiles, asps, and scorpions, into whose legitimate home the desert Christians had encroached to make their own place of residence. In addition, unfavorable weather might occasion drought or the failure of a crop upon which one relied for food. Taken literally, the exchange of question and answer about fear while walking in the desert refers to the desert environment in which every step might yield a hazard. Solitude under these conditions was risky. If a person fell ill or was unable to obtain water, death was a real possibility in a place where such isolation brought one closer to the utter reliance on God these desert Christians seem to have wanted to realize. Part of the attraction of the desert environment was that it was a place of such physical vulnerability, which allowed one not only to rely on God's providence for food and water, but even to develop relationships of mutual sustenance with neighbors and pilgrims. The creation of a network of men and women checking up on one another and expressing care for one another as they did constitutes one way in which this literature might still speak to people's spirituality today.

Women, of course, might have their own particularly gendered reasons for experiencing anxiety about their material safety. The late antique world was a dangerous place for women. A story about a desert Christian named Apollo explains that as an "uncouth shepherd" he was curious about how a fetus grew in the belly of a woman, so he murdered a pregnant woman to find out, tearing open her body to see how the baby lay in her belly (Apollo 2). It should probably not surprise us that the focus of this story is Apollo's conversion at the age of forty, when this act was done, and the contrast drawn between his exemplary life and his criminal past. His whole subsequent life, indeed, is passed in compunction over the murder of the woman and her unborn child. The brief and tragic story ends with another old man reassuring Apollo of God's forgiveness, despite the persistence of his grief. This reassurance is significant as it reveals the interpretive authority that men themselves claimed for themselves and let each other claim, in terms of interpreting God's attitude toward such violent and sinful actions.

But what of the woman in this story? Where was she that she was vulnerable to Apollo's attack? If he was a shepherd at the time, we can probably assume he didn't meet her as an upper-class woman in an urban context, whose pregnant condition would have kept her safely in her own home with servants and family members to provide for her every need. Indeed, we are told he saw her in a field, where possibly they both were working. Further, Apollo likely met a *poor* young woman whose pregnancy was the result of abuse, for we hear of no husband or father or defender of the law who sought to avenge or even complain about the woman's death. Apollo is left unmolested the rest of his life, save for the rumblings of his conscience. The woman, of course, remains nameless— she and her child discarded as objects used to satisfy a man's curiosity. Naturally, this story should horrify us. And we should be gratified that Apollo himself is stricken with horror at what he has done. But is that enough? This woman is one of many unnamed desert daughters/mothers whose presence in the sayings collections seems only to serve a man's making progress in his own spiritual life—this particular woman's death serving a purpose by which Apollo was "converted."

Though it feels reductive of the woman and child to consider them symbols, it is meaningful to do so when they can thus function to remind us of all the women and children sacrificed by the male desert Christians in late antiquity who understood familial relationships to be detrimental to a man's "advancing to spiritual perfection." And it is also worth thinking about the fact that Apollo kills a *pregnant* woman in this story in order to understand the mysterious power a woman has to bear for nine months a child in her womb and to deliver the child, a power to give life that is not enjoyed by men. The exercise of Apollo's strength to dissect the woman to understand intellectually a life process from which he, as a man, was excluded indicates why other men may have treated women scornfully—destroying them, or attempting to do so—as compensation for their lack of this living power women hold.

What the story also lets us perceive is a valid reason for women to feel quite a bit of anxiety in the desert, when such things as this man's sating his curiosity about women were possible. Women have long been vulnerable to men's objectification in this way, and they had things to fear—not only for their lives, but also their general well-being. These both have often been in men's control. Women who dressed as men to survive in the desert become an increasingly common feature in the desert literature, as these women strategized ways for themselves to survive—to elude men's curiosity about and violence toward them. Disguised as "one of them," these women were able to elude notice. When, for instance, Bessarion and Doulas first visited an old "man" in his cave on their way to Lycopolis, they were rebuffed by the "man's" silence; on returning again to the hermit's cave, they discovered the hermit dead and that she was a woman (Bessarion 4). They use the situation to contrast women's ability to "triumph over Satan" with the men's violence they had witnessed in the city. And while this appears to be a favorable endorsement of women's lives in the desert, the fact that the men are surprised and impressed speaks to men's assumptions about what women are capable of.

Curiosity and astonishment that a woman could have lived incognito as a man and appeared as valorous as a man in her ascetic performance is worth noting, as well, and men's interest and curiosity is thus revealed as directed toward that which differs from them: not only revered men whose wisdom placed them in a location where less-wise men wanted to approach and learn from them, but also women as an even more fundamental other.

Sources of Desert Anxiety

Part of what might constitute a non-material, spiritual, or existential anxiety that emerges in the desert literature arose because men knew in some way that they were alienating themselves from the original gospel charism, but they were powerless to keep from performing this alienation. Tracing the movements associated with Luce Irigaray's "wandering" of man from himself,[3] this alienation was a process already in effect within the Greco-Roman context from which the early Christian desert movement came. As men, and some women, kept to the primary path of ascetic renunciation already espoused by the Greeks, Stoics, Cynics, and so on, they were keeping to a path of wandering from themselves that did not cohere with—and may have been in obvious contrast to—what they understood Jesus calling them to. As Irigaray writes,

> Men speak and speak to one another starting from a universe, cut into words and concatenations of words, parallel to the living world from which the logos divides more and more. They communicate by repeating, not by saying what is present here and now—of the world, of themselves. Hence comes a combination of self-importance, drowsiness, and anger. Men are no longer there where their discourse places them. *Between what they say and what they live, more or less fully, a part of them wanders.*[4]

Sayings attributed to Poemen indicate recognition of this wandering and express instruction to achieve harmony between

3. Luce Irigaray, *In the Beginning, She Was* (New York: Bloomsbury, 2013), 83–112.
4. Ibid., 85–86. Italics added.

being and doing: "Teach your mouth to say what is in your heart" (Poemen 164) and "Teach your heart to guard that which your tongue teaches" (Poemen 188). Indeed, sayings of this kind may be in continuity with the gospels themselves, interpretation of which might have been constituted to respond to and allay the wandering of man already in effect by the time Jesus lived and into the next few centuries, and even up until now.

This spiritual anxiety might have to do with simply lacking discretion, seemingly the most important virtue of desert Christian life (as the most sayings in the Systematic Collection are collected under this topic) and the most difficult to cultivate. One story documents the question, "How am I to find God?" After various suggestions are offered, an elder reminds the listener of the primacy of discretion: "Many have indiscriminately afflicted their flesh and have come away empty, with nothing accomplished. Our mouth stinks from fasting; we have learned the Scriptures by heart; we have perfected [our knowledge of the Psalms of] David, and yet we do not possess what God is looking for, that is, fear, love, and humility" (Discretion 135). This exchange documents a fundamental psycho-spiritual anxiety: that a person might do all he could to live perfectly the desert life and still lack something. Indeed, this expresses a fundamental anxiety regarding how to live out the life of discipleship Jesus called his followers to, an anxiety that every subsequent generation has seemed to feel a need to reformulate and address for themselves. In the desert Christian context, this anxiety might have had to do with the feeling that the desert Christians, in some way, "misunderstood" God's message in and through Christ, and had not lived into the fundamental reality that Christians were invited to: that of sharing God's unconditional love.

Such anxiety led to specific experiences of gynophobia and misogyny. However, it also led more variously to the tempting thoughts that form such a major concern of most characters in the sayings collections. These *logismoi*, or tempting thoughts and emotions experienced by the desert daughters and sons, were often attributed to demonic forces against which the desert Christians might prove their worth—thus, they were in some way necessary for the constitution of self.[5] These anxieties might manifest as any of the seven or eight "deadly sins," which Evagrius Ponticus famously catalogued and placed in a hierarchical schema, from least to worst in seriousness: gluttony, impurity (lust), avarice, sadness, anger, *acedia*, vainglory, and pride.[6] "Wandering" from himself, the desert son reinforced the dualism of body and soul and, as Irigaray writes, "even his way of taking care of himself becomes dual: gymnastics of the body or exercises of the spirit."[7] The desired antidote to experiences of anxiety about interacting with and being influenced by such *logismoi* took various forms, bodily and mental: experiences of interior stillness (*hesychia*), tranquility (*amerimnia*),[8] or repose (*anapausin*). Such experiences were cultivated by remaining present to the disturbance of anxiety and letting it dissipate. The desert tradition had a finely-tuned psychological awareness of how such tempting thoughts and anxiety about their emergence could grip the imagination: "When not being stirred up," Nil taught, "every passion simply progresses gently to what is more moderate and later completely ceases, in time forgetting its own activity" (Hesychia 23). Anxiety had to do with whether one trusted or doubted that such a passion might dissipate through natural

---

5. This is the main point of David Brakke's *Demons and the Making of the Monk: Spiritual Combat in Early Christianity* (Cambridge, MA: Harvard University Press, 2006).

6. Evagrius, *Praktikos*, §§6–14.

7. Irigaray, *In the Beginning*, 90.

8. For a sensitive treatment of this particular form of inner silence, see Tomáš Špidlík, *Prayer: The Spirituality of the Christian East*, CS 206 (Kalamazoo, MI: Cistercian Publications, 2005), 324–25.

means, or whether the self would be capable of engaging and "mastering" it.

Thus, there were diverse reasons for anxiety. Some were cultural-specific and have less meaning for readers of the Christian desert tradition today. But some other reasons might still explain contemporary anxiety: not understanding how God might want our lives of Christian discipleship to unfold, etc., expecting there to be one answer by which all else coheres. These aspects of anxiety might allow us to think about its usefulness: rather than seeking to alleviate it to achieve the *hesychia* so desired of the desert sons and daughters, might it be necessary to address the legitimate reasons for anxiety, especially when they are expressed by marginalized populations whose distress operates as a barometer for what might be wrong in a society? Anxiety would not, then, be a matter of God's will, except as it helps a person identify something that could be addressed and changed. Whereas the desert Christians seem to have believed God willed a person to feel distress—otherwise, a person would not desire to be different, symbolically expressed as entering the Promised Land (Sorrow for Sin 45)—such a belief must be tempered with the realization that anxiety might be a natural response to a deepened awareness of life's perplexities and human injustice.

Thus, anxiety in the Christian desert tradition was not just about whether one would be able to succeed in governing wayward impulses (*logismoi*), as much as this concern does appear foremost in the stories exchanged by desert sons. Anxiety was also about whether this desert way of life was really an appropriate way to be a disciple of Christ. Though Jesus did say his burden was "light" (Matt 11:30), how was that to be understood? Many of the desert sons may have reached the end of their lives still not having satisfactory answers to the questions: "Was this life worth it? Have I been saved? Is God pleased with me?" They lay, unfortunately, on their deathbeds, needing their disciples to console them or requiring a vision from God as confirmation of some certainty they might pass on to their equally anxious disciples. Such assurances were often given—or so the stories tell us. Characterized as having struggled all their lives to attain an elusive wholeness, these men were found on their deathbeds to continue the struggle (Advancing 25) and to even seem appalled at the waste they might have sensed their lives had been. On the other hand, stories are also told about how joyful some men were to meet death, to be seen as "migrating" on further into no-man's-land (Advancing 15) and to even anticipate possession of knowledge withheld from them during their lifetimes. These kinds of stories must have offered solace not only to those the onlookers told but also to later readers of these stories, who themselves were dedicated to a life in pursuit of spiritual knowledge and experience at the expense of their cultivating true being and becoming.

Gynophobia in the Christian Desert Tradition

What was gynophobia in the Christian desert tradition all about? In the stories already related, we see men who relate to women as hindrances to their own spiritual development and as an object of mystery to be "dissected." These stories reveal complex assumptions and worldviews that are not easily dismissed as gynophobia or misogyny, and yet I will characterize men's anxious relations with women in the desert sayings as both. Existentially, gynophobia proved a parallel to the desert anxiety toward the divine and the diabolical—and the uncertainty they occasioned when one did not have confidence in one's own powers to discern between them. Similarly, gynophobia had to do with fear of the uncontrollable, of the one with generative power beyond male comprehension and experience. Theologian Catherine Keller identifies *tehomophobic* elements in the Hebrew and Christian Scriptures, as the redactors of the scriptures—men—expressed and repressed fear of the "womb" in associating it with dread powers of the cosmos and chaos.[9] This kind of fear is evident in the literary legacy of Christian thought, as men—its principal producers—register fear of the feminine.

However, this is not to say that women inspire fear. Rather, this is to say that men fear their own lack when in relation to women: their own lack of fecundity, their own lack of control over their own sexual desire, and so on. When focused on the *mother*, as it often is in the desert sayings, this fear expresses a fear of recalling one's origins, of having experienced radical physical contingency in relation to another—not God in this case, but a woman. A secondary fear derives from this: that one may lose control of oneself and again experience such radical physical contingency and *enable* a woman to become mother through sexual relations with her. The self-control a man might be thought to be cultivating in the desert alone was always shaky; indeed, stories tell of elderly men still experiencing unwelcome sexual urges late in life. And if we consider sexuality an important dimension of human life, we can sympathize with these men—and women—caught in a lifestyle that lumped many forms of ascetic renunciation into a single expression of Christian life, rather than respecting the diversity that is woven into the very diverse tradition that the Christian desert might represent if we look closely enough at it. Adopting a lifestyle that was in some ways "unnatural" to oneself resulted in anxiety and subsequent gynophobia and misogyny directed toward the ones thought to occasion such anxiety. For instance, one saying tells, rather pathetically:

> A brother was travelling. He had his own mother with him, and she was an old woman. When they came to the river, the old woman was unable to get across. Taking his own shawl, he wound it around his own hands to prevent him

9. Catherine Keller, *Face of the Deep: A Theology of Becoming* (New York: Routledge, 2003).

from touching his mother's body. Carrying her in that way, he brought her over to the other side. "Why did you wrap your hands, my son?" the mother asked him, to which he replied, "Because the body of a woman is fire and from proximity with you would come the idea of another woman." (Self-Control 83)

This saying has supplied part of this chapter's title: the claim that a woman's body is fire. Though the implication here is that fire is dangerous, fire is multivalent in the sayings. Not only might it be associated with, on the one hand, demonic temptations, and on the other hand, the Eucharist and the words of the gospel,[10] but it can indicate something either divine or human—in both cases, potential danger. When men appear "like fire," in the fingers or the face or more generally, this manifestation accompanies prayer and seems to evoke memories of Jesus's transfiguration (Matt 17, Mark 9, Luke 9). For instance, famously Joseph's fingers became like lamps of fire as he explains to Lot that he can become all flame, if he wills (Joseph 7). Other stories speak of the countenance or the whole being shining with fiery light. It is difficult, however, to see how this particular desert son's words about his mother's body indicate this quality; instead, this quality is not divine but coupled with intensely human feelings, suggestive of something the son considers dangerous to himself were he to come into contact with his mother's body. The overlap of fire, however, used as a natural element to signify qualities both demonic and divine is telling, and it demonstrates a similar quality of repulsion and attraction resulting in anxiety around discerning a right relationship with this source of simultaneous repulsion and attraction, demonic and divine.

Granted the traditional assumption that stories of this kind had something to teach future men and women committed to monastic life, we can see the wisdom expressed in this

---

10. See *The Book of the Elders: Sayings of the Desert Fathers*, trans. John Wortley, CS 240 (Collegeville, MN: Liturgical Press, 2012), 75, 337, and 341.

brother's observing the power of memory. However, moving beyond this assumption, we can also observe the woman's role in the story to prompt her son's expression of wisdom. Her seeming lack of knowledge is remedied by his answer; but we can ask: is "lack of knowledge" the only thing her question indicates? Might it also indicate confusion, criticism, and even consternation, as well? Unable to understand why her son refuses physical contact with her, this woman dares to ask him about his actions, putting him on the spot to explain himself—to explain why, while providing her with needed assistance, he has also needed to take thought for himself and his future fallibility should contact remind him later of other women he might also think of. It is worth remembering this woman's being deprived of the touch of her son, as an act he initiates for his own welfare and not in consideration of hers. Such family members, often female, reappear in the sayings, never quite as aloof as many of the desert sons may have wanted their stories to show.

Furthermore, what exactly is exemplary about this brother's act of self-preservation? Its indication that the brother understands the gravity of proximity and what proximity to any woman—even an aged woman and even a family member—might lead to relates to the kind of thing any celibate person might have issues with: how, for men, to control proximity to women, not only those who might prove tempting with whom to have a physical relation with, but those of one's own family. This story seems to legitimize how future generations of men desiring cloistered, solitary existences with other men might say to the women of their own families, those who might express confusion, criticism, and even consternation about their decision to remove themselves from proximity: "Leave us alone." And, indeed, to feel comfortable with themselves saying this, because it ostensibly leaves them with a safeguard against future temptation. And yet is that all it does? No. It also allows men their own privacy and relinquishment of the difficult work of becoming in communion with the gendered other with whom they might have had a meaningful spiritual life, and the difficult work of co-creating a spiritual life with and for the other.

Phobia And Deference

While the preceding story tells of a man's attempt to distance himself physically by means of a cloth he put between his own body and the body of his mother, other stories tell of more subtle circumspection oriented toward others. Thus, it would be naïve to consider phobia as only extended toward women; with the instruction to maintain no friendship with a woman was the instruction to maintain no friendship with a child— meaning, a young boy with whom, also, a male person might be induced to sexual activity (Advancing 34). Indeed, another saying characterizes the ruin of four churches in Scetis for their permitting young boys to join (Isaac 5). Whether or not women exchanged similar precautions in their spiritual teachings, or experienced the same kind of qualms, we have little knowledge. One saying does, however, recall a woman living with others who falls sick and when her brother comes to visit, *she* refuses *him*, as "it was unacceptable [for her] to see a male person" (Self-Control 52). She sends word to him via another to the effect that she believes they will meet again in heaven someday, deferring their meeting in the flesh. This resembles too closely other refusals by men to see their female family members for us to know much about the woman's actual feelings. All we are told is that the woman's piety is tied to her keeping herself aloof from male company. This story is offered certainly as a lesson for future female readers who might be tempted to interact with men, even family members. And this avoidance, in duplication of men's ideals, expresses a woman's piety and safeguards her status as a consecrated virgin.

Another story not only documents a man's fear of his mother, but also his reverential awe for his mother and respect for her good opinion of him, itself rather charming in a collection of sayings that seemingly disown such orientations:

An elder told how a youth who wanted to retreat [into the desert] was impeded by his mother. But he did not abandon his project, saying, "I want to save my soul." Much as she tried to stand in his way, she was not able, so, in the end, she let him go. Off he went and lived alone in a disorderly way, wasting his life away. Now it came about that his mother died; then, some time later, he himself became gravely ill. He fell into a trance and was whisked away to the judgment; there he found his mother with those who were being judged. She was astonished when she saw him. "What is this, my child?" she said. "Have you too been condemned to come to this place? Where are the words you used to say: 'I want to save my soul'?" Bowled over by what he heard, he stood there dejected, having nothing to say in reply to her. Then, by the providence of God, the lover of folk, after seeing those things, he made a recovery from the illness that was afflicting him. Reckoning that a visitation like that might have been sent from God, he shut himself up and stayed there, concerning himself with his own salvation, repenting and weeping over the things he did previously in a disorderly way. Such was his sorrow for sin that many begged him to relax it a little, lest he do himself some harm by his excessive weeping. But he would not be comforted: "If I could not endure the reproach of my mother," he replied, "how then am I to endure being put to shame before Christ and his angels on the Day of Judgment?" (Sorrow for Sin 38)

While we may want to be careful to relate what we understand of maternal sensibilities now with what we read about in the sayings collections, we can distinguish some comparable elements in this story: the mother's concern for her son and the son's concern for his mother. These reciprocal concerns might be said to resemble that shared by other parent-child pairs. Here, however, maternal care is distinguished by a woman desiring to block her son's retreat into the desert. We do not get details as to how she attempted to do this; we get evidence, however, of her failure, though tempered by the words "in

the end, she let him go" as if there were some kind of permission the son still sought of his mother before insisting upon
his own way. Significantly, this departure is spoken of by the
man as the means by which he will save his soul; when presented with such a motive, it might be hard for a mother with
any amount of agreed-upon authority to stand in a son's way.
The woman might have blocked her son's project out of selfish
concern, and yet this woman's resolve might equally indicate
wise understanding of her son's project as misguided, that
other means existed by which the son might "save his soul."

The story tells us the mother died, and afterward the son
had a vision or experienced some kind of anticipated judgment
where he found his mother. The information relayed by this
part of the story is descriptive of the mindset of those at this
time period who seem to have expected the virtuous not to
await judgment: thus, the mother is surprised to find her virtuous son accompanying her in the wait for judgment. Evidently,
he is unable to respond to his mother—being rendered speechless is not uncommon in dreams, especially those evoking terrifying emotions—and when he recovers, the son commits
himself to compunction and reformation of his way of life. We
are told at the end of the story that his not ceasing from lam-
entation over his sins is motivated by a recognition of relationship between enduring the reproach of his mother and the
shame he anticipates he could experience at divine judgment.
This gynophobia is specific: oriented toward the mother and
evocative of the shame a son could feel in not having performed
the distancing of himself from his mother that natural human
maturation and healthy human functioning require. Instead,
he remains linked inexorably to a phantom mother whose judgment serves as a surrogate of divine judgment. This is the kind
of link with family relations that the ascetic life was supposed
to sever; that it did not wholly do so serves as a useful loophole
and counter-tradition indicating the persistence, even in one's
own mental landscape, of mothers.

As terrifying as the reproach of the mother seems to this repentant son, it is telling that the story ends with his juxtaposing—and seeming to make a practice of doing so, whenever someone urged him to relax his excessive weeping—avoidance of his mother's reproach with that of divine judgment, implicitly valuing the latter more and devaluing the former. Reflecting on his own capacities, the son creates a sequence by which he characterizes himself as insufficient to meet the lesser obligation and, thus, to be in need of strenuous repair in order to meet the more demanding obligation. Thus this story presents the maternal in an ambivalent light, positive in one way and negative in another.

This particular form of gynophobia—a son's fear of his mother—is perhaps not what we would expect in the literature: the typical form being that of a woman whom one might oneself make a mother—the temptress female. Certainly there are many more stories of this latter kind. However, I find this story about the mother particularly illuminating because it shows a process of laying the blame of one's failure to achieve the holiness the male ascetic set out to achieve as the fault of one's mother or, perhaps more accurately, as the fault of one's still harboring uneasiness around the fact that one *had* severed one's relationship with one's mother. It is certainly curious how often women as mothers appear in this literature. However much a man might have wanted to abandon remembrance of his having been born of a woman and relied upon her feeding, teaching, and caring for him in his younger years, this was not wholly possible. Indeed, when we think about Origen, whose theological and ascetic influence on the desert tradition is impressive, we ought to remember the particular relationship his mother had with him—that she is principally responsible for his not achieving his object of being martyred. The historian Eusebius tells us how close Origen came to ending his life but for his mother's taking action, inspired by "divine and heavenly Providence": realizing verbal chiding in terms of "spar[ing] a mother's feelings" was not enough, she went further than the mother whose story was related above in taking action to prevent her son's "saving his soul" by hiding his clothes, disabling his venturing into public space where Christians were being persecuted under Emperor Severus's direction.[11] If this mother-son relationship is not often recalled while celebrating Origen's contribution to early Christian theology and scriptural exegesis, we may even more familiarly recall Monica, a known and named mother, when we consider Augustine. The formative influence Monica had in her son's conversion and the presence she persistently offered her son was despite his attempts to get away from not only her but also the feminine represented by his mistress. Finally, even that Jesus and Mary enjoy an important relationship in subsequent Christian history and tradition allows us to sense that there is something important going on in these mother-son relationships that the desert tradition is at pains to repress. And, yet, scriptural precedent indicates even more severity around these relationships than we might often remember. The next section will recall this precedent to our minds in order to understand the trajectory set by Scripture for familial relationships within the Christian desert context.

Misogyny in the Christian Desert: Scriptural Antecedent

When we encounter gynophobia in the sayings, we are encountering a powerful phenomenon of male existence. In some ways this phenomenon is more powerful than hate. However, hate is not absent. Hate arises from fear, in the sense that because one despises oneself for fearing, one becomes

11. Eusebius, *The Ecclesiastical History, Volume Two*, trans. J. E. L. Oulton (Cambridge, MA: Harvard University Press, 1973). Origen's history is detailed in book 6 and his mother's actions in section 2.

hateful toward the "object" that inspires fear. It is radically unfortunate that hatred of kinfolk is enshrined in the New Testament teachings, as Jesus teaches: "If anyone comes to me and does not hate his father and mother, wife and children, his brothers and his own life, he cannot be my disciple" (Luke 14:26). My impulse here, however, is to question the legitimacy of the claim that Jesus himself taught this. The teaching certainly coheres with other teachings that shame equivocation, or "counting the cost" of discipleship; but it promotes a radical disjunction between Jesus's demonstration of divine love toward those who shared or did not share his own cultural, religious, or gendered identity. Biblical scholars have also speculated that this kind of gospel teaching reflects a later conflict between Jesus's disciples (engaged in missionary work throughout the Roman Empire) and his family members (associated with James in Jerusalem), and the various antagonisms that arose between these groups. By having Jesus "disown" his family members in this way, those communities siding with the disciples could promote their own message of salvation in contrast to what Jesus's family members in Jerusalem maintained.

Because of Scripture's profound influence on the desert Christians,[12] we must problematize teachings like these, and ask whether they are there because they suited the purpose of those early male Christians who wanted to call into question the authority that *women* had in Jesus's life—not only his

---

12. As Douglas E. Christie writes, "In the desert, Scripture's surplus of meaning endured not in the form of commentaries or homilies but in acts and gestures, in lives of holiness transformed by dialogue with Scripture. The sacred texts continued to mean more not only to those who read or encountered the texts but also to those encountering the holy ones who had come to embody the texts [the desert Christians]. The holy person became a new text and a new object of interpretation." *The Word in the Desert: Scripture and the Quest for Holiness in Early Christian Monasticism* (New York: Oxford University Press, 1993), 20.

mother and siblings, but also his female followers. Is it not useful to those male readers and leaders of faith communities in the early centuries, and even beyond, that Jesus expressed disdain for family members? It provides a justification for them to do so, as well. "The definition of Christian is the imitation of Christ," reads one succinct desert saying (Advancing 37). But other aspects of displaced familial loyalty in the gospels must be acknowledged as well, as potentially serving as a foundation for the kind of gynophobia and misogyny we find in the desert tradition and subsequent Christian tradition. Whether or not these episodes in the life of Jesus are authentic it is impossible to say and perhaps many feminist readers like myself would like to believe they are not. The teachings fundamentally oppose the inclusivity found in other parts of his teachings and they function to ostracize and censure women. For instance, another passage tells:

> Then his mother and his brothers came; and standing outside, they sent to him and called him. A crowd was sitting around him; and they said to him, "Your mother and your brothers and sisters are outside, asking for you." And he replied, "Who are my mother and my brothers?" And looking at those who sat around him, he said, "Here are my mother and my brothers! Whoever does the will of God is my brother and sister and mother." (Mark 3:31-35)

Here we see Jesus affirming the "kinship" of those who follow him and who do the will of God. It is obvious that he has had to avoid affirming any men among his followers as "his" father and thus we are left with the familial relationships of mother, sister, and brother to characterize his followers, reinforcing of course the patriarchal image of God as Father. It is also worth noting here that Jesus's pedagogical process is to ask a question and answer it himself, not giving his followers any leeway for answering mistakenly or for answering literally a question he intended to be taken metaphorically. Certainly, spiritual kinship is not negligible in the history of Christianity; however, when affirming spiritual kinship, especially in the form of teacher-student relationships, becomes a means to disown physical relationships, it becomes problematic.

Another biblical exchange is even more damaging, in that it has to do with a one-on-one encounter with and direct rebuke of a woman: "While he was saying this, a woman in the crowd raised her voice and said to him, 'Blessed is the womb that bore you and the breasts that nursed you!' but he said, 'Blessed rather are those who hear the word of God and obey it!'" (Luke 11:27-28). Again, Jesus subverts the acclamation—here voiced as blessing of Mary, who may or may not be present, whereas we know her to be standing nearby in the Markan episode related above—by refusing to endorse it, and substituting something else in its place. The woman's testimony regarding Mary is refused by Jesus, and she is disciplined to be trained in another direction: as his other hearers must be, as well. We are to consider blessed those who hear and obey the word of God. However, is it not curious that that is exactly what Mary did, in accepting the terms of the annunciation, hearing the words, "You shall be with child" and affirming, "so be it"—isn't this exactly what Jesus's interlocutor is making tangible through her raised voice? Isn't her calling it to Jesus's attention and to the attention of those in the crowd a means of not only affirming Jesus's status, but also a reminder (though rebuffed) of Mary's importance, and the importance of every woman-mother "behind" the figure of exemplary, wise men?

That Jesus had a mother is undeniable, though Scripture may present him as downplaying the relation in favor of the genealogies and kinships he was, himself, inaugurating with a "kingdom of God." As such, he was progenitor to figures like Mary Magdalene, to whom he entrusted the message of his resurrection, instructing her to inform the other disciples about his status. In doing this, Jesus is revealed as one who may subvert the cultural paradigm of male privilege, and certainly the gospels retain traces of the uneasiness the disciples feel in becoming participants in a subverted order of this kind. Yet this uneasiness did not lead to affirming women's status within the community of believers, but quickly collapsed into expressions of distrust, anxiety, gynophobia, and misogyny. These expressions result eventually in attempted erasure from the story, and the necessity for readers now to attend carefully to this process of erasure in order to reconstruct what was there that was not attended to and, when noticed, erased.

Renouncing Family in the Christian Desert Tradition

Having briefly surveyed familiar biblical texts that speak of severing familial relations in favor of "doing the will of God," it is instructive to note that the Christian desert tradition made little explicit use of these texts. Though the transfer of allegiance from physical, familial relationships to the metaphorical will inform our reading of a similar "metaphor-making" of women in the desert tradition in the next chapter, for now it is enough to note that of all these biblical texts, the first about hating one's family members appears *only once* in the desert sayings. And, curiously, it is cited by a woman.

An extended story in the Anonymous Collection tells of a beautiful and astute woman—unnamed of course—married to a rich merchant (Anon 84). When her husband dies, a colleague of his named Symeon shows interest in marrying her. She arranges a "test" for him to reveal where his true desire lies: after requiring that he fast for an exorbitant period of time, she meets with him and invites him to choose between a table set with food or the bed in which he might enjoy her body. The choice is clear, of course, and the woman uses this opportunity to instruct the man that even though they may have mutual love for one another, they may renounce it in order to please God, per Jesus's teaching about identifying disciples among those who hate family members. Symeon immediately puts her plan into effect and the story ends telling us how he became an exemplary monk. The story says nothing about the woman's own "happily ever after," and lacking that, we may assume that Symeon did not know what happened to her but told the story about himself to explain the origin of his monastic vocation. Another option, of course, is that the woman's action in the story and her citing of Jesus's teaching was, for her, a form of self-preservation—to remove herself from a situation in which she did not want to succeed in becoming the wife of another merchant. Whether or not she married someone else, or remained widowed—allowing her widowhood to enable her to live an independent life as many wealthy widowed women of her time did—is impossible to know. But her astuteness is highlighted in the text, and we can see her exercise of it as securing her a future that she wanted. Scripture, and even a text that promoted severing of personal relations, was a tool for her use, in this respect.

Though this story in the Anonymous Collection is the only explicit citation of one of these biblical texts, another saying addresses what must have been a common experience of lamenting severed familial relations among the desert communities:

> If you have renounced the things of the flesh for the sake of God, do not let indulgence draw you while you are residing in your cell into lamenting father or mother or the love of brothers, the tender affection of sons or daughters, or the love of a wife. For you have abandoned everything for the sake of God; so recall the hour of your death and that not one of those persons will be able to help you [then]. (Watchful 118)

Certainly this troubling saying operates by virtue of its appeal to one's self-interest, that one only makes decisions about interacting with others based on what they can do for you. In the case of family members, because they will not be present at judgment to speak for one, they must be abandoned and one must assume sole responsibility over preparing oneself to appear alone and speak for oneself before such a judgment seat. This is certainly a warped vision of salvation, though perhaps still familiar. The saying characterizes grief over the loss of family members as self-indulgence in order to persuade the reader against expression of these experiences. Further, we know this kind of saying to be addressed solely to men as the words "or the love of a wife" indicate a culture where heterosexual marriage was the norm.

The fact that men are shown valiantly resisting such love, as well as the "tender affection" of offspring, illustrates two things. First, many of these desert Christians had been married, had had children, and had abandoned them. And, yet, these men are the exemplars of the early Christian ascetic tradition! No wonder such a literature can exasperate contemporary readers. Second, as do so many of the sayings, this teaching exhorts recollection of death in deliberate contrast to memory of the one who gave birth to one, the ones to whom one might have helped give birth, and the woman who gave birth to one's children. The flourishing of the family and the contribution a man might make to it is supplanted in this tradition by the cultivation of remembrance of death. Such cultivation is not unique to Christianity; it was already part and parcel of the Greek philosophical tradition and formed an essential component of "spiritual practice" as determined by those for whom philosophy was a "way of life."[13] And yet when accompanying and even precipitating gynophobia and misogyny, we have to wonder if these ways of interpreting Jesus's life and ministry were the only ways to do so.

13. See "Learning to Die" in Pierre Hadot, *Philosophy as a Way of Life: Spiritual Exercises from Socrates to Foucault,* trans. Michael Chase (Malden, MA: Blackwell, 1995), 93–101.

To be fair, there were other sayings advocating alternative uses for the natural sorrow one felt at abandoning one's family. For instance, when asked whether a desert son should consider his parents, one elder responded: "Whatever consideration you know brings tears to your soul, spend time on it and, when weeping comes, then graft it wherever you will, either onto your sins or onto some other good reflection" (Anon 548). This is lovely, in that the elder is not advocating a cessation of the natural feelings that a man would have in following a masculine-formed path into the desert—indeed, nobody was forcing these men to live these lives!—and yet his advice is that the sorrow not be exorcised so as to change something about the cause. The man is not permitted to return to or even consider what he might owe his parents. Instead, his sorrow is to be utilized for other purposes, "grafted" onto other places of his life where sorrow is expected and perhaps hesitant in appearing, such as reflection upon one's own sins. This dynamic is one of pretense and is one I explore elsewhere as "holy feigning," a strategy whereby desert Christians might use duplicity skillfully to grow spiritually. This is one dimension of that holy feigning whereby a person might "pretend" his real emotions were about something they were not about.

The main problem with sayings of this kind is that the logic presented is so narrow: as if one may only experience sadness about one thing at a time. Or, as another saying puts it: "the love of humans often separates us from the love of God" (Anon 556). This saying also posits a logic foreign to contemporary female readers, as if one might only have one love-object, or have only a limited amount of love to be distributed to specific people, and that one must—and can!—make determinations about how this love be distributed. This law of scarcity and demand hardly applies to something so dynamic as love.

A final story about a desert son and his mother will illustrate the severing of familial relations that this literature was at pains to advocate and explain:

> There being a severe famine, [the devout brother] took some loaves and set out to bring them to his mother, and here there came a voice saying to him, "Is it you or I who looks after your mother?" In acknowledgement of the point the voice had made, the brother threw himself face down on the ground, begging and saying, "It is you, Lord, who cares for us," then he stood up and went back to his own cell. Then, on the third day, his mother came to his cell, saying, "Such and such a monk gave me a little grain, saying, 'Take this and make us some little loaves so we can eat.'" The brother glorified God when he heard this. He was suffused with hope, and, by the grace of God, he made progress in every virtue. (Discretion 137)

Interpreting this "voice" as divine reproof is certainly convenient for this particular brother. Having proof of God's provision by means of another monk's giving his mother surplus grain, the devout brother's responsibility to his mother is dispensed with. This story comes from a lengthy chapter on discernment, so we may assume that it is ostensibly about that very important desert virtue. The brother has learned to discern how he himself is expected to live given how he "reads" God's action on behalf of his mother. It is impossible to overstate how ridiculously convenient this is for the man to not have to worry about his mother anymore. Whose voice is this, exactly? Is this indeed a divine reproof directed at a man who presumed to take over God's responsibility? Or is this rather the expression of a man's wishful thinking that he be legitimately allowed to live apart, on his own, with no social responsibilities distracting him from his sole purpose of attaining personal salvation? And, we may ask, what kind of salvation is this that demands its recipient focus so exclusively on his own metaphysical status, rather than the physical well-being of familial others who depend upon him?

Woman: The Desert's Mirage?

The ultimate fantasy of the male subject in the Christian desert was that the desert landscape be absent of women. And, not only that the outer landscape itself be devoid of women, but that men's interior landscape of memories and imagination be devoid of women. Thus, when the desert elder, Abraham, suggested that he and a friend move closer to civilization, the other resisted, asking instead to be taken where there might be no women. Where, the question emerges in the saying and in the discourse between the two men and their collective fantasy, might no women be? The desert (Hesychia 26). While we know this was not true of the Christian desert, this story preserves the hope that it be true in revealing the desire on behalf of male subjects that they be able to live free of women's presence—a desire we've seen demonstrated and acted upon in other stories. This story provides evidence that no matter one's age and a supposedly waning libido, one might still have trouble in the presence of women. And this trouble is not necessarily limited to the sexual. I suggest that such distress comes from the visible and intellectual reminder of the paucity of the tradition of male aloofness that was emerging at this time, and its having been inherited from centuries-old philosophical traditions resulting *not* in the well-being sought by men. The radical invitation of inclusivity that the gospel was supposed to have offered humanity seemed to be thwarted in the first centuries of Christian life, and I believe that these men knew that and suffered from that knowledge. Women served as an inconvenient reminder of mistaken steps. Indeed, a radical dissonance remains evident in this literature documenting men's experience and I claim that dissonance arose as men intuited the failure of their own systems, devoid of female presence. This intuition was not the way they were taught to validate knowledge, so it went unexpressed and dislocated from its real source. Eventually, men will elaborate systems of existential angst, dread, and mystery in relation to the divine in order to explain to themselves why anxieties remain in their lives, non-integrated with female companionship.

The desert location that assumes physical and metaphorical importance in the sayings collections and lives of the desert sons and daughters suggests an important image that might serve as a useful backdrop for the exploration of women's lives in this book. For some men, this desert location suggests the possibility of outrunning the physical presence of women, because women were tied ideologically to a cultural context in which they might best bear and rear children. The desert consisted of dunes and shifting sands, rocky hills and salt mines, and of trackless wilderness. As we make our way through the stories derived from experience in such seemingly inhospitable surroundings, we note that many of the women whose lives we consider in this book left no visible footprint; indeed, some of these women—associated with demonic forces—appear as phantasms or mirages in the desert context. The persistence of such imagery suggests that something integral to men's spiritual existence and even vitality involved women. Though the typical interpretation of this literature has been to see men resisting distractions in an effort to mature spiritually, it could be that the distractions themselves and the forms they took for men have something to teach us—and something that could have taught the desert sons themselves—about how spiritual maturation occurs.

For instance, Poemen warns about trusting one's senses too much, describing how a man who thought he saw a copulating man and woman urged them to stop, even making contact with them to separate them, only to find what he took to be the couple was sheaves of corn lying in a field (Poemen 114). That men might see features of the landscape in this way—erotizing their desert home—suggests an impressionable aspect of their past interactions with women. This story of Poemen's friend mistaken about the couple having sex in a field seems to confirm the absence of physical women in the desert with whom a man might be sexually active, and yet it also emphasizes how a movement was afoot in men's experience to displace the physical with the metaphysical. Women's physical presence was seemingly obliterated while remaining viably present in men's conscious thoughts, memories, and even influencing their physical actions, including violence toward physical elements of their surroundings—in this case, corn. That this aspect of their surroundings be corn is significant as well in anticipating later ecofeminists' articulations around identifying women's degradation and oppression and the earth's at the behest of patriarchy—because of a significant commonality related to the earth and to women: that of providing sustenance. So, though a man is also depicted mistakenly in this sheaf of corn, the sexual act itself is more poignantly represented by the presence of two: an act of physical sustenance as meaningful to human well-being as that of the corn itself.

This question of interpreting one's experience is important and as we consider possibilities, we learn more about the frameworks available to us which suggest more favorable "readings" of experience, which might change over time as our frameworks alter. For instance, one desert story relates how a child, growing to be a man in the Christian desert alongside his biological father, was bothered by "forms of women" that appeared to him by night (Porneia 25). These apparitions are certainly a kind of "mirage" in the sense that no physicality is adduced. The storyteller reports as fact the demonic source of these apparitions, drawing on a worldview shared with the early reader about the externalized nature of temptation. This is certainly one possible interpretation of a story of this sort, or of any of the stories involving demonic figures. We are not going to be able to argue whether this child who became a man experienced certain things or did not. What we can suggest, however, is that, given another worldview, this experience might be interpreted as a man's memory of his mother and of other female family members or companions of his mother who, before he was weaned, were a part of his world, only to vanish once the boy and his father went to the desert.

The story continues that in going into villages, the boy—now grown to be a man—sees women for the first time and confesses they are the ones who troubled his childhood imagination and we can assume his later adult dreams. His father misleads him by not admitting they *are*, in fact, women, and instead calls them "monks" of the villages as opposed to monks of the desert. Just as the father is amazed at the persistence of woman in the subconscious of the child, so the reader is expected to feel astonishment and fear at the power of such unbidden and innocent memories. Nowhere is man able to escape this exposure, not even in the desert waste itself, not in a solitary cell, not within the "shelter" of the master-disciple relationship,[14] not in the privacy of one's own thoughts. Nowhere can man eradicate from his memory the experience of having been born of a woman. Peripherally, we might say, the boy's mother does appear in this story along with those who may have accompanied and assisted her in childbirth and in early infant care of the boy, though these women are conflated with demonic forms. A complex psychology is revealed when a different worldview frames the interpretation of these stories, questioning the legitimacy of men's resistance to and avoidance of women in the Christian desert.

14. Irigaray, *In the Beginning*, 4.

The Manipulation of Woman: Creation and Destruction

A few final stories further demonstrate how men participated in the manipulation of woman for their own sake, both fearing and hating women as the external manifestation of their own unwanted feelings. Indeed, abstract "woman" served as a tool for relating to these men's own desire for the feminine, rather than allowing them to recognize the particulars of individuals they might have known. In the first story, an elder shapes not only a woman out of the clay to create a physical substitution for the insubstantial tempting thoughts he continues to have, but also a baby daughter for whom he could "play at" being responsible:

> Abba Olympius of the Cells was tempted to fornication. His thoughts said to him, 'Go, and take a wife.' He got up, found some mud, made a woman and said to himself, 'Here is your wife, now you must work hard in order to feed her.' So he worked, giving himself a great deal of trouble. The next day, making some mud again, he formed it into a girl and said to his thoughts, 'Your wife has had a child, you must work harder so as to be able to feed her and clothe your child.' So, he wore himself out doing this, and said to his thoughts, 'I cannot bear this weariness any longer.' They answered, 'If you cannot bear such weariness, stop wanting a wife.' God, seeing his efforts, took away the conflict from him and he was at peace. (Olympius 2; parallel in Porneia 50 with unnamed elder)

Of course it is significant that the child this man "engenders" in play is female. She and her clay mother represent the seemingly insatiable demands of the feminine from which these desert sons fled. While it is exemplary in some ways for this man to have "exorcised" these feelings of desiring female companionship in ways that did not actually affect other living beings (as the man in the previous chapter did in sending away his wife and child in order to become Poemen's disciple), it is troubling to consider how disposable this man considered such relationships to be. Easily constructed, manipulated or played with, and then dismantled when not seen to be consistent with his *true* objective of living a life of "repose," these manmade "objects" within his experience trivialized not only the mother and daughter he might in actuality have had but trivialized also his desires, rendering them easily managed and disposed of through internal dialogue and feigning.

Later in Christian tradition, Saint Francis is said to have experienced much the same internal conflict and resorted to the same engagement with natural elements to shape for himself substitutes for a family of which he deprived himself. Instead of clay, Francis used snow and these snow figures, silent and immobile as they were, schooled him in relating to his desires.[15] Whether or not Francis's hagiographers were aware of this desert son's story and drew on its simultaneous severity and play to speak of their own tradition's revered founder is impossible to say, but the creation of outward manifestations to interact with as a playful consequence of one's desires—to test the waters of one's acting on desire and rehearse experientially the outcome of doing so in this way is poignant indeed.

Another story in the same chapter on *porneia* a word indicating not just physical acts of sexual gratification but the desire for such acts, tells of the memory of a woman, beloved of a desert disciple, whose death enables him to manage and eradicate his persistent desire for her. Indeed, it is notable that intellectual knowledge of her death does not cause his desire to cease—indicating what many desert dwellers must have

---

15. Thomas of Celano, "The Remembrance of the Desire of a Soul," in *Francis of Assisi: Early Documents Volume Two: the Founder*, ed. Regis J. Armstrong, J. A. Wayne Hellmann, and William J. Short (New York: New City Press, 2000), 325. I am indebted to my friend, Stephen King, OFM, for calling this story to my notice and providing me with this reference.

noted as the "irrational" dimension of such temptations. Even in light of the woman's death, this particular man feels he must take measures to secure himself. The story tells:

> There was a brother fighting the good fight at Scete, and the enemy put him in mind of a certain most beautiful woman, cruelly afflicting him. Then, by the providence of God, another brother came down from Egypt to Scete, and as they were speaking together, he said that the wife of so-and-so had died: the very woman on whose account the brother was embattled. On hearing this, he took his *levitón*, and going up to Egypt by night, he opened her tomb. He mopped up her bodily fluids with the *levitón* and returned to his cell with it. He would set that stench before him and do battle with the *logismos*, saying, "Look, the desire you are pursuing: you have it before you, take your fill!" In this way he tormented himself with the stench until the warfare ceased from him. (Porneia 26)

The woman's bodily fluids taken to the desert as a visceral remembrance of the disgust which this particular brother felt toward his own feelings for this woman indicates a particular relation to woman that the desert tradition was to make suspect. This brother who mops up the woman's bodily fluids with his own clothing seems perhaps even thus to "wear" her stench. At least, he carries it back to the desert with him, letting its "presence" abide with him in his dwelling.

It is undeniable that the desert sayings are marked indelibly by gynophobia and misogyny. However, it is somewhat gratifying to examine the literature closely and note that there are few stories of such overt gynophobia and misogyny as those attached to this body of literature. What is there is appalling, certainly; however, accounting for the presence of such attitudes can do much to mitigate the effect of these stories. The contemporary female reader of the sayings, learning to understand why men expressed fear and hatred of women and why the literature documents these expressions, can look with sympathy on such men and check their own resistant impulse to throw out the whole of the sayings because of the presence of repellant male attitudes. Recognizing and accounting for gynophobia and misogyny also serves to enable us to question the agenda of the sayings and to recover the reality that the sayings were, at times, at pains to keep covered: not only women *were* present in the Christian desert but that they led successful lives there, successful according to standards erected by men, but also potentially successful on their own merits. We, unfortunately, know less about what women might have thought themselves about their own lives; however, that lack of knowledge invites us to engage our imaginations and consider what unnamed women, women who are peripheral to the main thrust of the narrative of the sayings, offer contemporary readers of the sayings.

One final story tells how:

> a woman who had something seriously wrong with her hand came with another woman outside the window on the north side of [Longinus's] cell, looked in on him, and took note of him sitting there. He reproved her saying, "Go away, woman," but she remained [there], watching him but saying nothing, for she was afraid. He realized and became convinced what was wrong with her. He got up and shut the window in her face, saying, "Go away, woman; there is nothing wrong with you," and she was healed from that hour. (Wonder-Working 7)

This is a curious story. It tells about two women in company, one with something flawed about her hand. They both sit outside this desert son's quarters, though quickly one woman becomes absent from the story. Only the flawed woman remains, persistent to receive a healing. The rebuff Longinus offers, similar to that of Arsenius when the woman from Rome visited him with which we began this chapter, is not accepted by the woman. She remains watching and inaudible, a truly contemplative moment with a woman powerful enough in her silence to effect change in her life through soliciting a source she believed able to help her. Remarkably, she is able to effect this change through presence and not verbal plea. The narrator reports on the woman's fear, though there is no evidence of that in the story itself. Longinus's wonder-working is the focus of this story, as indicated by its inclusion in a chapter on "wonder-working." Thus, his intuition of her need enables him to heal her, though inadvertently. He persists in his desire for her to leave him, and so he claims there is nothing wrong with her, which, if not true before, is now true in his voicing it. His speaking the truth into existence is the site of wonder-working in this story. He closes the window on her, asserting "There is nothing wrong with you."

I end this chapter with this saying because it is a provocative one. Two points stand out to me: First, female readers today are invited to be tenacious contemplative witnesses of the unjust severance of relationships that men manufactured for their lives in the Christian desert tradition. Looking persistently at the tradition—not averting our gaze, though we are unwelcome visitors—we can, in fact, force the tradition to admit this truth: there is nothing wrong with us. Indeed, if we merely visualize the events of the story, we have no certain indication of Longinus's power or virtue, only of his rudeness and desire to maintain his solitude apart from women. His inadvertence in speaking a salvific word to her may also speak to female readers of this literature today: "There is nothing wrong with you." Though many of the male characters in this literature subscribe to a view that there is something seriously wrong with women (in not being men), this particular affirmation from Longinus inadvertently speaks the truth. In recognition of the woman's trauma, he is the one to reverse it by speaking it. We might still object that this affirmation is effected by Longinus and his word was powerful to effect change, when what we really want to hear is a woman's affirming and effecting this reality for herself. However, I find it important that such "cracks" in the façade of male privilege in the literature persists, through which we can see men's real anxiety, fear, and hatred toward others so different from themselves, and yet not wrong for being different.

CHAPTER THREE

The "Disappearance" of Women into Speech

The last chapter ended with the image of mirage to suggest how men engaged their imaginations to govern their own sexual impulses. They did so by constructing phantasms of women, "born" in a sense from repressed memories and exteriorized as phantoms they might actively resist. These endopsychic projections are meant to suggest that women themselves were not physically present in the desert, that they were replaced by these "others" with whom men might courageously do battle and over whom men might triumph. Such a lack of women's physical presence is shown to be patently false by other stories, as has already been shown and will be further shown.

Nevertheless, women's seeming "absence" from many of the stories of the desert must be accounted for, and one means of doing so is by looking at the discourse exchanged by men, replete with metaphors drawn from women's bodies and experience. Why do we find such metaphorical constructions? Especially in a body of literature that advocates the resistance of thoughts and memories associated with women? One answer might be that it acted as a kind of "release" mechanism, enabling some kind of stabilization among men who were essentially de-stabilized by their self-sequestration from family. We might also consider that men appreciated something about the female body and women's maternal experience, so much as to incorporate such imagery into their own speech patterns and teachings. A further answer might involve insisting on men's usage of such language as a violation of women's experience, especially when used to characterize negative things and to uphold soul/body, female/male, human/divine dichotomies contemporary to this late antique world and continuing to influence readers today.

In whatever way we account for these metaphors in the desert literature, the task of this chapter is essentially to trace the "disappearance" of women from physical to metaphorical status within the "world of the text," the text being that of men's discourse. By no means do I want to give the impression that I buy into the narrative that women were absent from the desert context, but I do want to advance the notion that if they seem absent this is truly only a seeming. They were there, and some of the evidence of their continued presence may even be suggested by the ubiquity of feminine imagery in the discourse exchanged by men. These traces allow us to not only affirm women's presence in these men's lives but also to resist the impulse to believe, along with what the text advances, that men were happier and better off without women. The "disappearance" of women into speech functioned to give men a place where their natural thoughts about women might find space for elaboration rather than be suppressed.

In this chapter, I begin by considering two stories that speak of women silenced and erased from the physical domain of the desert but, more importantly, from men's company and the literature about them. The subsequent sections in this chapter deal with how men continued to speak of women between themselves, though coded in metaphor and analogies. Women's bodies themselves were not to be thought of, and yet remnants of such memories remain in the stories and teachings the desert sons exchanged with one another. By focusing on men's experience, I am still primarily approaching my topic of ways of love in the Christian desert tradition in a "deconstructive" mode, as in previous chapters, before moving on to the reconstruction of women's presence in the desert alongside men, resistant to such reality. However, these stories provide meaningful evidence of men's appreciation of women and women's experience as a means of communicating about their own spiritual lives that meant so much to them.

The implications of the men's silencing and erasure of women for our own time should be obvious: such dealings with women have resulted in contemporary exclusion of women from many domains of experience including possession of material wealth, political and religious leadership, and elaboration of women's own processes of achieving and maintaining psychological wellbeing. Similarly, men's appropriation of women's experience to speak between themselves echoes into our contemporary centuries when we consider the persistence of gendered language to speak of the soul and even of the church. Elizabeth A. Clark writes of research conducted on the recovery of female biblical imagery when referring to Sophia, or Wisdom. Though empowering to many faith communities oriented toward inclusion and even celebratory of women's leadership, this Sophianic imagery was actually utilized, according to Howard Eilberg-Schwartz, to alleviate men's anxiety around homoerotic relationship with the divine when the latter was figured as male.[1] The same might be said for what we find in the early Christian

---

1. Howard Eilberg-Schwartz, "The Nakedness of a Woman's Voice, The Pleasure in a Man's Mouth: An Oral History of Ancient Judaism," in *Off With Her Head!: The Denial of Women's Identity in Myth, Religion, and Culture*, ed. Howard Eilberg-Schwartz and Wendy Doniger, 165–84 (Berkeley: University of California Press, 1995). Cited in Elizabeth A. Clark, "The Lady Vanishes: Dilemmas of a Feminist Historian after the 'Linguistic Turn,'" *Church History* 67, no. 1 (1998): 26.

communities' discussions. A linguistic explanation is possible for both biblical and desert traditions, in that words for wisdom (the Hebrew *hochmah*, the Greek *sophia*, and Latin *sapientia*) are female; the neuter is used for the soul (*pneuma*) and the feminine for the condition of quietness (*hesychia*) used by the Greek writers of the desert sayings. Acknowledging this linguistic explanation, I yet move beyond it to demonstrate the bias of this literature toward excluding women from conversations and spiritual experience shared by men and its strategy of enacting this bias through not only terminology—that is, merely words associated with women—but imagery of women's experience.

The Disappeared Woman

Before examining strategies of transporting women from physical embodied presence to the realm of verbal exchange, I comment on two stories from the collection of anonymous sayings that illustrate well the concern men had with women's *real* rather than imagined presence in the desert, and their strategies for dealing with this very real presence. The first of these stories contains straightforward instructions for dealing with the "necessity" of interacting with women. These instructions are succinct and twofold: a man is not to let her say much, and if the man has to say anything to her, he is to speak sparingly and then dismiss her quickly—lest her smell remain to "contaminate" the man's thoughts (Anon 506). We certainly see Longinus behaving this way. "Go away," he tells his female visitor not once, but twice. But how might other desert Christians have come into contact with women, given the impression the texts offer that women were not in the desert? Ostensibly, they might interact with women in the marketplace where the men may have ventured to offer handmade wares for sale, or through acquiring food, water, or materials for handwork from women in the same place. However, the suggestion in this instruction of dismissal is telling. Paired with the previous instructions about the goodness of persevering in one place and of learning to live alone by first living with others, this instruction creates a scenario in which a man remains where he is after having *dismissed* a woman—as if his solitary cell is, in fact, the location of meeting.

How would this be possible, unless women, too, were among those visiting the men in their solitary retreat and later in their communal, protomonastic dwellings, such as Longinus's visitor does? Such a woman might have been a disciple seeking spiritual companionship or instruction (see Anon 518, for instance), a pilgrim visiting from an urban center (remember the rich widow who visited Arsenius), a woman sharing the same watering hole for laundering (see Porneia 47), a family member visiting or seeking help (see Porneia 28 and multiple sayings), a "disreputable" woman intent on proving she could tempt an anchorite into sexual activity (see Porneia 42). Or, indeed, she might be a neighboring ascetic, elaborating her own spiritual journey within her own solitary cell and also venturing out to share resources with a desperate neighbor. Any of these possibilities substantiates women's physical presence in the desert and could account for the elder's characterization of such interactions as a "necessity," incurring an obligation for reticence on the part of the desert son.

Curiously, none of the various stories mentioned in the previous paragraph record men acting quite in the way this elder advises: "Do not let her say much. And if you speak [to her], sum it up in a few words and quickly dismiss her" (Anon 506). On the contrary, these men engage the women and, respectively, disdain their virtue, rebuke them for visiting, engage in sexual activity, welcome a visitor to stay with them, and indeed invite them to spend the night. An internal conflict between desire and disdain for women, real attraction to and engagement with women as opposed to the cultivation of distance and reserve with women seems to be at play here, inviting us to consider such "cracks" in the façade of consecrated religious life created by the texts of the desert sayings as evidence that not all was as it appears in the desert context or as men wished it might be.

Another crack appears in earlier questions voiced by this same anonymous disciple. This particular teaching concerning women appears as the answer to the third of three questions posed by an unnamed brother of an unnamed elder, the first being, "Is it good to live in the desert?" and the second being, "How can a man live alone?" The first of these questions may surprise us, given the assumption voiced in the literature that it *is* (of course!) good to be in the desert. But such assertions and such questions as this one, posed to elicit an affirmation of the desert as the site of spiritual transformation, do suggest doubts on the part of some listeners. The inquirer here seems to feel the need to verify this value of the desert and to ask how one might accomplish living there alone suggests, also, how difficult that may have been, and how—from this man's personal experience—he needed another to confirm what could have seemed misguided to him—and, indeed, to many others. The saying succinctly addresses central values of the desert literature: the location of the desert enables exceptional experiences of material deprivations and also of contemplative awareness of God's presence; solitude is necessary for taking responsibility for engaging one's own personal demons, "in single combat against the adversary" (Anon 506), having been schooled already in the difficulties of interpersonal affairs with other desert sons; and women are to be silenced if present, cautiously spoken to, and summarily dismissed—as detrimental to the men's spiritual formation.

In an androcentric document like *The Sayings of the Desert Fathers and Mothers*, we cannot expect this saying to encompass what it means for women or even for all men to be spiritually formed. It is addressed wholly to men and takes only men's situations into account. For women's needs, we will have to look elsewhere. For now, it suffices to attend to how the saying acknowledges the real presence of women and strategizes ways to keep her in abeyance. A second story enacts more explicitly the erasure from the desert that men seem to have wanted to effect through their forming bonds of solidarity with one another. A short statement, this saying simply reports that a man happening upon a woman's footprint on the road as he walked along, bent over and covered it up, explaining his action as concern lest a fellow male desert dweller happen along also and have tempting thoughts (Anon 430). That this man apparently had no tempting thoughts himself is neither suggested nor denied. The story is preserved for its exemplary expression of concern for another. "They said . . . ," it begins and one is left to wonder whether the man had traveling companions who later reported the incident from firsthand observation of the incident, or whether the man had been traveling solo and told others later about his action. Either way there is intention expressed by the man's action and intention expressed by the fact that we have the story at all.

Indeed, what is particularly interesting about this saying is that it does nothing to "cover up" men's "covering up" of women in the desert. Such actions are assumed to be virtuous in a literature that is primarily concerned with men and their anxious concerns related to creating the ideal habitation for achieving and maintaining their own spiritual well-being. The action in the story may be taken literally, as the act of covering up the woman's footprint obscures evidence of the woman's actual presence in the desert. It may also be taken figuratively, as a symbol of the "wiping away" of women's presence in the desert and in their own psyches that men hoped their desert location and ascetic/contemplative practices would make possible.

Both of these stories illustrate men's strategies for "effacing" women—whether a woman who, though present, was not permitted to speak and was sent away or a woman who, previously present, has all visual evidence of her presence eradicated by a man's gesture. Indeed, the latter story indicates in a superb manner how mere material evidence of the woman's embodied presence was threat enough to require immediate action; many other stories indicate the threat a woman's body might pose for the desert sons. On the other hand, the former story may surprise us in fixing women's threat in her voice. In fact, the instruction of this story regarding not letting a woman speak is important in indicating what may have been seen as a more significant source of threat: women's expressing a testimony to a way of Christian life that counteracted that adopted by desert sons, suggesting alternatives to their own modes of solitary existence.

Both strategies of silencing and erasure demonstrate men's exerting control over their environment, including women as a feature of that environment. And while both strategies evince a mode of self-preservation, the strategy of erasure depicts complicity on behalf of the male population in the desert: that they would obscure, for one another, any suggestion that women remained in their vicinity. Naturally, this is represented as a token of kindness or thoughtfulness but emerges, for women readers, as conspiracy to participate in a "cover up" that effectively denies the existence and value of women's lives in the Christian desert—either in pursuit of their own spiritual formation, or as companions to men there.

These two strategies may strike contemporary readers as puerile—as boys not letting the girls "play ball" with them. As we get into the next chapter and its examination of gendered competition in the desert, we will see why it may have seemed necessary not only for women to adopt rather extreme ascetic practices in order to advance spiritually along lines set out by men. We will also see why men seem to have thought it necessary to keep women at arm's length, as they identified these powerful women as threatening their own sense of self-worth in addition to being responsible for arousing their own sexual instincts.

The Soul as Maternal

Even as men wanted to obliterate women and the memory of women from their physical locales and interior landscapes, women's presence asserted itself among them even more strongly—a dynamic not unfamiliar to those schooled in basic psychology. What is repressed is damaging, and it will emerge in some form or another. Denied archived presence in most of the literature of the desert tradition, women nevertheless continue to show up in its discourse exchanged by men. In this way, they are, in part, "exiled" from the tradition: represented as bodily absent (for the most part) and yet conceptually present.

Unable to erase the feminine fully from the desert, men used language to co-opt women's generative capabilities. They do this by making female experience into a metaphor they might appropriate for the description of their own experience to express (1) the soul and its work and (2) the generative quality of the peace and quiet they sought—a peace and quiet that they seem not to have associated with the kind of life they could have had with a partner and children.

In the next sections, I describe ways in which the soul appears "maternal" within the desert literature and then demonstrate how the desired peace and quiet, known as *hesychia*, was also conceptually presented as maternal. I seek to show that women were never far from men's thoughts and from their discourse with one another. Even when they exchanged words concerning biblical interpretation and applying biblical wisdom to their own lives, they focused on the female. One example of this focus appears when Poemen explains why temptations recur to the desert sons: they fail to guard their name and status. He cites the Canaanite woman of the gospels who was heard and responded to by Jesus when she persistently asked for help (Matt 15); he also cites David and Abigail, when Abigail takes upon herself the guilt of her husband's lack of hospitality toward David (1 Sam 25). Poemen reduces Abigail to a symbol of the soul and David to a symbol of God: "So when the soul accuses herself [as Abigail did] before the Lord, the Lord loves her" (Poemen 71). This kind of equivocal valorization of the female as demonstrating the exemplary gesture of humility before God reinforces an equally present exclusion of the female from representation of the divine. The hierarchical gender relations common to late antiquity (and that remain common to this day) are reinforced by this kind of use of the Bible to speak of men's experience in the desert. However, my main point in introducing this story here is to point out how consistently the desert sons used the figure of the female in their discourse with one another. These women never really disappeared, not in person and certainly not in speech. They were present as biblical exemplars and present as embodied female relatives, friends, and neighbors. Though we have scanter evidence of the "disappearance" of women in person, we have ample evidence of the latter.

To show the pervasiveness of femininity in the discourses exchanged by men indicates again an uneasiness these male desert Christians may have felt about their pursuit of the Alone alone and how such a pursuit in the form of the lifestyle they adopted in the desert might not have wholly reconciled with what they understood Jesus to have called his disciples to. That some men might have been legitimately called to a life of solitude is undeniable; however, the enthusiasm for the movement that motivated more men and women less suited to this vocation to adopt lifestyles that removed them from the transformative possibilities of social life in married relationships and in families took Christian discipleship and even spirituality in a direction that was unnecessary and indeed damaging.

Though apparently foreign to the desert sons' experience, married relationships and families entered their discourse and teachings when speaking of their own experience. This is shown in a teaching exchanged by Longinus and Acacius:

> A woman knows she has conceived when she no longer loses any blood. So it is with the soul, she knows she has conceived the Holy Spirit when the passions stop coming out of her. But as long as one is held back in the passions, how can one dare to believe one is sinless? Give blood and receive the Spirit. (Longinus 5)

This saying opens with a concrete image drawn from women's experience of menstruation—a surprising acknowledgement that men of the desert knew women's lives intimately, as sons and brothers, friends and lovers. Menstruation, however, serves as a negative example when aligned with the soul that continues to have passions "flowing" out of it. The desert sons' passions are demonized when associated with the experience of a woman who can bear children, who, indeed, is ready to bear a man's child. This is a state of being "held back." The pregnant soul, on the other hand, demonstrates its responsiveness to the Holy Spirit as engenderer and thus operates as a goal at which the desert sons aimed. In a way, this association is surprising because, given the desert Christians' assumptions about sexual intercourse and its seeming to have no place in the desert, the actual fact of it having happened and occasioning conception works well here for Longinus to make his point about the soul's receptiveness to the Spirit. This teaching, in fact, articulates a tension within men's experience in the desert: that some aspects of women's lives might, in fact, be important for the men to remain a part of, despite the insistence on avoiding and even rejecting women.

Rejection of family members was not exclusively directed toward female family members, however. Men were enjoined to leave behind other familial relationships besides that of wife, sister, mother, or daughter and to adopt a new familial context within the desert setting: a man's spiritual teacher was "father" and his fellow disciples "brothers." These are important metaphorical moves made by the desert Christians and two things account for them. First, the Coptic words for father (*abba/apa*) and mother (*amma*) used of beloved elders was common among many of these desert Christians. Second, language of familial relationship was already in use in the first and second centuries to describe social ties among members in early faith communities (see Acts and the letters of the apostle Paul) to speak of the kingdom of God as a community of kinship inaugurated during and subsequent to Jesus's lifetime. In the desert literature, we find also a desert son's rebuke of a messenger reporting his father's death to assume this transference of loyalty. In making this transference, he affirms the immortality of his divine father in contrast to the mortality of his biological father (Advancing 5). Indeed, a saying such as that which tells of a brother boasting to Poemen that he eats a lot of vegetables (Poemen 186) and eliciting Poemen's disdainful reply that this does not help him, that he should rather eat bread and only a few vegetables, and to not return to his "father's house" or "relations" for what he needs[2] suggests that the ascetic impulse of late antiquity might have been reified by such an anti-family, anti-community orientation. Practices that enabled the desert son to avoid returning to or relying on his family meant curtailing dietary needs, as well as sexual needs; that this impulse might have contributed to the development of late antique asceticism is possible—as a way to make concrete one's severance from family and society of a certain kind.

While this transference of loyalty from biological to spiritual companions is striking, the preponderance of maternal meta-

---

2. John Wortley's newer translation of this saying in his *Give Me a Word* renders the former translation of "father's house," while Benedicta Ward's older translation uses the gender-neutral "relations."

phors in the sayings extends this transference. Not only were wise women and female spiritual teachers referred to as "*amma*," but the soul itself was deemed maternal. That the soul is metaphorically female has an antique pedigree, originating in gendered linguistic conventions (*pneuma* and *anima* are construed as neuter in the Greek and feminine in Latin) and accruing philosophical importance when serving to distinguish in Greek literary tradition the divisions of the immaterial dimensions of human being: mind (associated with the male) and soul (associated with the female). In the desert literature the attribution of the maternal to immaterial reality thus settled where we might expect it to settle—on the human soul.

Why this attribution? Or rather, why this reification of a symbol already familiar to those reared in the Greco-Roman tradition? To begin, the activity of a mother was known to most men who used this metaphor, and it could serve as an easy means of communicating through joint knowledge. Thus, when an inexperienced desert disciple admits to his tempting thoughts being more than he can bear, we hear an exchange like the following, functional because of the men's shared experiential knowledge:

> The disciple: What am I to do, Father? The impure *logismos* [tempting thought] is killing me!
>
> The elder: When a mother wishes to wean her child, she puts wormwood on her breast, and when the child comes to suckle as usual, it turns away because of the bitterness. If you are willing, you apply wormwood too.
>
> The disciple: What is that wormwood which I ought to apply?
>
> The elder: Recollection of death and of the punishments of the age to come. (Porneia 35)

Here we have a glimpse of a practice, of which the elder himself had experienced as a young child or he observed women in his own family to have done or he knew as women's wisdom. Whatever the vehicle of the knowledge coming to him, woman was the source. And he appears confident the disciple appealing to him will understand. That the tempting thought corresponds to the maternal breast, upon which the disciple must "smear" memory of death and punishment, is significant in a chapter on *porneia*, or habits of sensual gratification. Though it could seem counterproductive to evoke thoughts of a woman's "breast" in the imagination of the troubled disciple, the elder is seen as offering helpful advice in connecting a female body part to the disciple's thoughts and offering a theoretical "barrier" to thwart his engagement. Cultivating a habit of erecting such a barrier himself, the disciple may be confident that he will learn to turn away from such thoughts because of the "bitterness" of what he has come to associate with the tempting thought. This is not just a refocusing of one's attention, but rather a schooling of oneself to associate the undesirable with the desirable, thus "contaminating" the desired. Of course, the result is that women's bodies, too, as the desired are contaminated through association with the undesirable. This happens in another manner as well, in the stories that effect a general demonizing of women's bodies, associating the appearance of women whether physical or imagined as the work of a diabolical tempter to be resisted.

Striking, too, in this saying about wormwood as a metaphorical strategy is the advice that the desert son is to make of himself the nursing woman, treating another part of himself as the child to be weaned. A more spiritually mature desert Christian, Poemen, also uses language suggestive of mothers with their children when he refuses to interact with a visitor desiring to speak of Scripture and other spiritual things. When rebuffed, the visitor changes his discourse to the mundane—that is, to the persistence of passions in his day-to-day life. Poemen then becomes animated and endorses the visitor's purpose, saying, "This time, you come as you should. Now open your mouth concerning this [his troubled experience] and I will fill it with good things" (Poemen 8). The visitor is represented by Poemen here as the needy child, and Poemen himself is the maternal figure, either human or animal—both would fit his image of offering sustenance to the young one's open mouth. Indeed, this particular saying is useful evidence for my earlier supposition that men's discourse about the spiritual life was intentionally adopted to take the place of other socio-spiritual relationships, such as a mother enjoys with her child.

Just as these sayings speak of a mother and her treatment of a small child she wishes to wean or to feed, so other sayings represent maternal experience with offspring who wander. This is expressed first by Macarius in human terms and then by another desert son with a maternal image drawn from the animal world:

> Just as a mother gathers her own children together in the house, instructing and admonishing them, so ought the soul to gather up her own considerations from everywhere they are wandering, like her own children, even if they are scattered by sin, so as to gather up her *logismoi* constantly (to the best of her ability) and to await the Lord in firm faith so that, when he comes to her, he may teach her true, undistracted prayer directed solely to interceding with him. (Vigilance 49)

> Just as when an ass is tethered, her colt runs hither and thither, but no matter where it goes, it comes back to its mother, so too do the *logismoi* of one who waits patiently upon God in his own cell return to him again, even though they might roam around a little. (Patience and Courage 37)

Both sayings draw on the intimate relationship between mother and offspring, suggested possibly by Jesus's speaking of himself as a mother hen in relationship to the inhabitants of Jerusalem (Matt 23:37; Luke 13:34). Macarius speaks of the soul as an active figure, using the tools of the emerging monastic trade such as psalm-singing and compunction to discipline thoughts, and yet he implies this may not be enough with the inclusion of the phrase that this worker gathers thoughts "to the best of her ability." The second saying indicates the natural movement of thoughts to "return" if one only waits patiently. This saying expresses a profound psychological insight found elsewhere in the sayings and attributed to Nil: if thoughts are not actively stirred up, they simply dissipate (Hesychia 23). Here, the "patience and courage" evoked by the entire chapter of sayings in the Systematic Collection are advanced as strategies for waiting out one's recalcitrant, impulsive thoughts.

Whether emphasizing the activity or passivity of the human soul, both sayings speak of God, referring to divine collaboration with the soul. And here we may see one reason why it was so useful, as well as linguistically "natural," for the speakers within the desert literature to regard the soul as female. The soul is encouraged to wait for a God supposed male, a father-figure, who will come and teach the soul how best to commune most effectively with "Him." The activity of having one's thoughts gathered is incomplete without the appearance of God—as male—to effect "true, undistracted prayer" or "hesychia." Such anthropology is indeed convenient in reinforcing the patriarchal status of the divine in the desert literature. The desert sons interpreted the Hebraic tradition as well, as being in conformity with this framework, as when an elder taught:

> The Shunamite woman took in Elisha, [and she conceived and bore a child thanks to the coming of Elisha] despite the fact that she had no relations with any of the men [see 2 Kgs 4:8-27]. It is said that the Shunamite woman represents the soul, Elisha the Holy Spirit. At whatever time the soul withdraws from the disturbance and trouble of the world, the Spirit of God comes upon it, at which point it is enabled to bear fruit even though it is widowed. (Second Sight 34)

John Wortley also translates this saying as indicating the woman's "barren" status, rather than being widowed (Anon 363). The social implication is, of course, that a *widow* would have no occasion or opportunity to bear children, but *barren* more accurately describes the physical implication the saying is getting at. The soul needs the Holy Spirit just as a woman needs a man to conceive children: the metaphor of "fruit" is suggestive of what is generated in each relationship, whether virtuous action or a child. This elder could hardly be suggesting that Elijah had sexual relations with the Shunamite woman! However, the quasi-miraculous quality of what he did do serves to render this analogy apt for discussing the operation of the Holy Spirit with the human soul.

Again, it was convenient for the male desert Christians to think of the divine as male, associated with Elisha in this reading of the biblical relationship, and of the soul as female. Though "spirit" could be said to soften an explicitly patriarchal representation of God in this saying, the obviously gendered division of the human-divine relationship reinforces male supremacy and subordinates women to passivity—though tempered somewhat by the notion that withdrawal from disturbance is what occasions the coming of Spirit and the generation of fruit. Such withdrawal itself, as the catalyst for divine action, might be and was engaged equally by women as by men.

These metaphorical uses of the maternal to express the soul and to express how the desert disciple was to be spiritually formed suggest the usefulness of ordinary life and observation to speak of complex, intimate, and intangible realities. That the men chose to use language of the feminine is illuminating to indicate that women were in reality not far from their minds, if kept far from their habitations (which itself is questionable). It is also illuminating to demonstrate the pointed way in which such metaphorical discourse, when used to distinguish the divine and human, was used to buttress men's understanding and vision of themselves as superior.

Hesychia as Transgressively Maternal

The word *hesychia* is used to express inward stillness and silence and may derive from a Greek term indicating sitting. Hesychia was a form of meditative experience generated by stilling the body in order to still thoughts. Metaphors such as looking into stilled water to see one's face (Hesychia 29) indicate the cross-cultural understanding of mindfulness and recollection being advocated by the desert Christians as what makes self-knowledge and spiritual transformation possible.

One can see the naturalness of the maternal metaphor being applied to hesychia because its quality of embodied practice involved physical stillness, just as a pregnant woman may require stillness and peace for the healthy inward maturation of a fetus before birth. Indeed, a woman—Syncletica, one of the few named desert ammas—speaks of a quality of rootedness, repose, and contentment with or commitment to one's place as essential to one's faith, though—curiously—she is represented as speaking of an animal's experience rather than a human one: "Just as the bird that gets up from her eggs makes them infertile and barren, so the faith of the monk or the virgin who moves from place to place becomes chilled and dead" (Patience and Courage 22). Her inclusion of "virgin" in describing the reality of the one consecrated to religious life is understandable given her own gender, but her use of bird behavior rather than a woman's may surprise us. Perhaps it should not, though. Syncletica forbears to reduce her gender's maternal experience to a metaphor, instead choosing to use observation of bird life to her advantage in teaching, suggesting a continuity of experience between animal and human life. In this way, she also forbears to alienate her friends listening to her, many of whom may not have been mothers.

Indeed, *The Life of Syncletica* puzzles in part because its author demonstrates Syncletica as reclaiming much of women's experience for the late antique female who renounces social relationships of marriage and family. Syncletica is seen as describing marriage to the Heavenly Bridegroom as transcending marriage to a human being; she is seen as describing a fetus's experience in the womb as evocative of the human soul's progress through subsequent "births" and indeed to speak of Earth as a "second maternal womb" while reinforcing gender divisions between one's homeland and mother ("heavenly Jerusalem") and God the father.[3] Further, Syncletica makes of women's work including housekeeping and laundry a metaphor, reclaiming it for the spiritual soul work she and her friends were more concerned with. Whether this puzzling text represents women's experience of the spiritual life in the fourth and fifth centuries or whether it rather provides a counterpart to the *Life of Antony* for women readers written from a man's point of view is debatable. Nonetheless, its use of women's experiences as metaphors resembles strategies in the desert sayings collections surveyed here. Women, of course, have not vanished from the context of the *Life of Syncletica* into metaphors; and, it is likely that they had not disappeared from the context of the desert sayings collections either.

To return to consideration of hesychia, its maternal quality is explicit elsewhere in the desert sayings collections for its ability to communicate generation. The experience and achievement of hesychia was generative of a great diversity of spiritual gifts, as is indicated by the numerous metaphors in the "ode" to hesychia closing the chapter on this topic in the Systematic Collection:

> Hesychia is the mother of all virtues . . .
> O *hēsychia*! Mother of sorrow for sin . . .
> O *hēsychia*! Mother of gentleness . . .
> O *hēsychia*! Mother of all good . . .
> O *hēsychia*! Mother of devotion. (Hesychia 35)

---

3. Pseudo-Athanasius, *The Life of Syncletica*, 56–57.

Just as stability of place enables a person's spiritual fertility to act, so quieting of the body and mind within one's place generates all manner of virtues. Further, Diodochos expresses how hesychia may be generative more simply of wise thoughts when he explains, using imagery from the public space understood and experienced by at least some of the desert sons, that:

> Just as the heat quickly escapes outside if the doors of the bathhouse are continuously open, so it is with the soul when it wants to do a lot of conversing. Even if the conversation is good sometimes, its own heat dissipates through the gate of speech. So silence at the appropriate time is a good thing, being nothing other than the mother of wisest thoughts. (Hesychia 12)

One can see in sayings like this one how enamored some of these speakers were of using metaphorical language. Not only does Diodochos align silence with "mother" and the soul with a bathhouse, whose "heat" must be retained, he speaks as well of the "gate of speech." Each of these figures of speech demonstrate the communicability of seemingly incommunicable things—such as inward stillness and its cultivation—through mundane, tangible objects, people, and experiences.

Indeed, here the aspect of motherhood, along with that of "gate," helps Diodochos express the "appropriate time" he suggests that silence must be observed. Whereas a bathhouse to be effective might need its doors closed pretty much all the time, gates and mothers—especially mothers giving birth, as the generative quality of this metaphor suggests—evoke "appropriate times" in which they are closed or open, keeping a person or letting a person through or letting a fetus develop or giving birth to such a fetus. Discerning "appropriate times" could be an important part of a desert son or daughter's spiritual formation, and advice concerning discernment allows the desert sons to ostensibly avoid explicit prescription, though such freedom appears in creative tension with legislation concerning all the myriad forms of Christian life emerging during the third, fourth, and fifth centuries.

Another image aligning a young woman desirable by men to betroth and make the mother of one's children with the soul and evoking the experience of inward recollection is expressed by Arsenius:

> While a maiden is in her father's house, many want to be her fiancé, but if she starts going out, she does not please everybody. Some look down on her, others praise her; she is not held in the same esteem as formerly when she was hidden. So it is with the soul: if it begins to spread itself out, it cannot command the confidence of all. (Hesychia 11)

Arsenius's strategy here is certainly to advocate for the solitary lifestyle physically enacted by staying within one's solitary cell, which enables the cultivation of hesychia. Built into his teaching is evidence of social norms of the time, in which a woman might be more or less desirable to men given her habit of staying enclosed within her father's house or going abroad, respectively, the going abroad seeming to disperse the young woman's charms and energies that were better reserved for her future spouse. Men's possessiveness of their female partners is also implied by the lowered status a woman earned in having been seen abroad by others. Nevertheless, appropriating such social norms to their own spiritual state, such male teachers succeeded in not only feminizing their own experience but in excluding most women from the experience. In this way, the reality of women's existence was maintained but allowed to be controlled in discourse and dialogue so that most women in the flesh might be rendered out of place or merely superfluous.

Around the central image of maternal metaphor, whether speaking of the soul or as hesychia, arises a cluster of similar metaphors:

Agent of Possibility	Form of Containment	Result/What is made possible
desert disciple/God	practice of hesychia	virtues/devotion/ "the good"
brooding bird	egg	baby bird hatching
closed doors	bathhouse	heat, leading to cleanliness
maiden/patriarchal authority	house	esteem, leading to marriage

The typology suggested by the sayings in this section is that a kind of "form" is necessary to make something else possible, just as a female body makes possible the coming forth of a new life. Each of these relationships evokes a point of origin, or agent of possibility, in relation to a result, mediated by a "container" of some kind. The desert fathers understood maternity to stand aptly for such a container in their own experience.

Vicious Mothers

The desert fathers might be said to give equal weight to negative imagery associated with the maternal, in its possibility to suggest generative capabilities just as well as positive imagery. Not only using the metaphor to speak of virtues emerging from the experience of hesychia, the desert sons also spoke of maternal metaphors to suggest how vices operate. Thus, gluttony might be characterized as the mother of tempting thoughts of sensual gratification of other sorts, including sexual (Self-Control 80). Another desert Christian spoke of loose talk as the "mother of evils" (Vigilance 54). Along the spectrum of tempting thoughts elaborated by Evagrius, vainglory and pride stand at the furthest edge of those to be resisted by the experienced ascetic, and both vices are identified as well as the "mother of evils" (Self-Control 87 and Nothing for Show 6). Each of these metaphorical uses of the maternal suggest, as well, the relationship of possibility between something that originates and something that results, with women's bodies appropriated as a viable container for speaking of such origins and generations.

The double-sided use of the metaphor of maternity to suggest both positive and negative things could be said to suggest the equivocation with which men of the desert regarded women. My point in this chapter, however, has been to point out men's intolerance in the literature for women's presence while making use of women's bodies metaphorically to speak between themselves of their own experience, both anthropologically making sense of themselves as privileged human beings as men and pragmatically making sense of their experience of conflicted desire. That they chose a woman's body to speak of these aspects of their desert life suggests their desire to distance themselves from it—the choice of alien life experience, animal as well as female, demonstrates the desert son's amiability to consider himself in some way similar to the "other" as in being a created living being but enough different to hold himself aloof from susceptibilities associated with and observed of said "others." The "other" has been appropriated to explain an alien force or power not connatural to men themselves, against which the men are conjoined and conjoin one another to resist.

Before moving on to the next chapter, two points involving the "disappearance" of women into speech deserve further recognition. First, as has been shown, the use of metaphors involving female, and especially maternal, experience was appropriated by men to speak figuratively of their own experience. The actual woman as maternal—whether literally or metaphorically—was a common occurrence in the desert and, at least, in the men's experience in having been birthed themselves. Among the revered wisdom figures in the desert, we know of at least three women named in the Alphabetical

Collection of the sayings, and certainly more of them existed than are known by name. However, a correlation between fathers and brothers and mothers and sisters does not appear in the desert literature. Common usage of "brothers" to indicate male disciples not mature enough, spiritually rather than chronologically, does not correspond to similar usage of "sisters" to indicate women. Either they were known as mothers or not known at all.

Second, my decision to name this book desert daughters and desert sons reflects the scarcity of this kind of terminology that, nevertheless, suggests an important theological reality among the desert Christians. When considering these exemplary early Christian figures as mothers and fathers, metaphorically, we have tended to obscure the fact that many of them had *really* been mothers and fathers, and in obscuring this we allow a false image of the Christian desert to emerge. Not all of the characters who appear in the desert literature were celibate ascetics. To suggest a *spiritual* fecundity to their relationship with others is precious, in that it allows us to understand the importance of how others function in drawing out the spiritual "births" to which we are all called at various times in our lives. However, it also ignores the reality that these men and women were growing and being birthed themselves; and a more common identification—common in the sense of being shared among all the men and women, regardless of personal generative experience—is that of daughters and sons.

My suggestion that desert daughters and sons be used as commonly as desert mothers and fathers is not to promote the kind of familial God—often depicted as patriarchal—common in Christian tradition. Indeed, many feminists claim that designation of those in Christian faith communities as God's "children" keeps such members infantilized and dependent in a way that curtails their development. It is, rather, in continuity with patristic imagery of Christians involved in spiritually formative exercises such as those deemed "ascetic" as birthing themselves. As Gregory of Nyssa writes, "We are in some manner our own parents, giving birth to ourselves by our own free choice in accordance with whatever we wish to be."[4]

This metaphorical construction of relationship speaks to the "becoming" of our experience as never stabilizing in mere origination—mother or father—but continuing in eternal offspring: daughter and son. This usage also highlights the relational quality of Christians in communal formation, reminding us of the ways in which we are generated by others, and they by us. In short, such usage suggests to me a useful means of identification of desert Christians—and Christian readers of this literature today—as in dynamic process of spiritual transformation and without hierarchy of the sort indicated by "mother" and "father." The identification of "daughter" and "son" is more inclusive than that of "mother" and "father" and better allows the reader of this literature today, regardless of their own generative experience, to draw closer in understanding to the experiences of the desert Christians.

4. Gregory of Nyssa, *The Life of Moses*, trans. Abraham J. Malherbe and Everett Ferguson, Classics of Western Spirituality (New York: Paulist Press, 1978), 55–56.

CHAPTER FOUR

Competitive Asceticism

Women's Questionable Winning

S tories in the Christian desert tradition extol female virtuos-
ity in the ascetic life—and asceticism seems to have legitimately put women on a more equal footing with men than
they could have achieved by almost any other means; men are
often even shown at disadvantage when women accomplish
ascetic feats more astonishing than men's activities. In many
of these stories, though, women are seen as excelling at and
even exceeding standards erected by men. They are thus
shown as having appropriated male values, which allows the
masculine sensibility expressed in the story, even if upheld by
women, to achieve a sly victory. Women have succeeded and
even perfected men's performance of ascetic practice, but they
achieve such success on men's terms. A brief preliminary comparison of two sayings that extol a desert son's ascetic performance and a desert daughter's will open this chapter:

> They used to say of Abba Helladius that for twenty years
> he never lifted his eyes to see the roof of the church. (Self-
> Control 16)[1]

---

1. The Alphabetical Collection adds that Helladius spent these twenty
years in the Cells (Helladius 1).

This saying expresses admiration for a man able to control his senses so as not to be distracted from his primary purposes. The length of two decades is significance in indicating that this practice was habitual for Helladius and not a one-time achievement. The saying very briefly and succinctly conveys a value of early desert communities, and the location of church indicates that Helladius not only went to church but was so focused on his interior life there that, though he may have been tempted to look around while there, he did not.

Another saying contains nearly the same sentiment in the same format, indicating likely knowledge of the previous saying, though individual, length of time, and location are altered:

> They said of Amma Sarah that she spent sixty years above the river and never peeped out to see the river. (Patience and Courage 26)

Personally, I find this saying a poignant expression of women's adaptation of their cultural and spiritual lives to men's expectations and men's admirations. Whatever is meant by Sarah's restraint from peeping out to view the river, we can see that the story extols this behavior as "patience and courage." The length of time she was able to maintain this practice was three times the length of Helladius's practice. And the difference in location also serves to make her story a bit more exemplary than Helladius, in that it seems to pair a place of residence with a place of worship, the former being a place likely occupied more often than the latter, meaning that Sarah's achievement exceeds that of Helladius. In the drawing together of these stories, though, we can see how closely they resemble one another with the one about Sarah communicating a more astonishing feat because of the length of her self-denial and because of the location where it took place. Indeed, it is worth dwelling a bit more on the difference in location between these two stories, as the church was becoming a place where men were accruing more and more power. Helladius's disavowal of that power might be suggested by his keeping his eyes trained on that which is below him; however, he might also have functioned as a priest within that context and the temptations to look down on members of his assembly, to scrutinize the sincerity of their participation in the liturgical celebration may have been difficult to resist.

Authors of early Christian literature exhibit a marked fascination with ascetic lives. Not surprisingly, men figure much more prominently than women in such literature for a variety of reasons, not least of which was the common association of asceticism, both etymologically and metaphorically, with athleticism. Indeed, it has taken a long time for women to be recognized as able competitors alongside men, as shown by the relatively recent (1970s) legislation passed in the United States as Title IX. Palladius of Helenopolis, however, encountered scores of female ascetics as he journeyed through Egypt, Palestine, and Syria in the late fourth century. These women offered challenges to men, including ostensibly to Palladius himself, and to each other just as they, in turn, were challenged by men and each other. Every ascetic's individual journey of faith was illuminated by its relationship with what the ascetic saw and knew of the other, both those within a network of specialized ascetic practice, comprising one's neighboring desert daughters or desert sons, and those without such a network who journeyed to places where ascetics lived in order to view their bodies and ascetic practices, such as fasting and sleeplessness, which resulted in literal transformations of the body.

To move from the desert sayings collections to a contemporaneous text that functions a bit like these collections in being anecdotal in nature about the various desert sons and daughters the author met or learned of, we consider in this chapter Palladius's *Lausiac History*. Palladius's *Lausiac History* upholds the potential of mutual edification ascetics offered each other, gender notwithstanding. In upholding such potential, he uncovers comparison and competition as activities to which Christian ascetics were prone and how these activities positively contributed to increased self-understanding and subsequent transformation. Not only did the ascetic exercise discrimination in seeking out a spiritual amma or abba, having thus to compare an elder's holiness against both him- or herself and against other possible candidates for spiritual mentorship, the ascetic also repeatedly engaged in comparison and competition in order to gauge their own progress in the spiritual life, such progress being revealed by the degree of conformability the life and practice of such an ascetic showed in relation to a recognized elder.

But *The Lausiac History* also contains stories of ascetics who compare themselves to and compete with one another and these activities frequently result in serious undermining of personal identity; in this way, we might characterize such competition as a questionably useful activity. However, because these stories demonstrate that an accumulation of self-knowledge occurred in the process means the experiences they describe are endorsed by Palladius as beneficial both to the ascetic undergoing them and to whomever might witness these events, including readers for whom Palladius compiled his *History*. In his Prologue, Palladius offers sensible advice: readers should avoid those "who can be no help to you" and to consider his book an opportunity to meet "holy men and women so that you may see clearly your own heart. . . . The comparison will enable you to see your own sluggishness or indifference."[2] Undermining of selfhood by comparison, though potentially permanent in its effect, might only be pain-

---

2. Palladius, *The Lausiac History*, trans. Robert T. Meyer (New York: Paulist Press, 1964), 28. Subsequent citations from *The Lausiac History* will occur within parentheses in the text with chapter and paragraph numbers from Meyer's translation.

ful temporarily, and, therefore, Palladius defends it as a positive good. The act of comparison entailed scrutiny of the other's praxis, not gender, and for this reason it was natural that Palladius include women's stories in his *History*. However, to show that women, no less than men, might challenge men (and other women) was not Palladius's only reason for their inclusion. He also affirms women's ability to experience the same self-revelation and transformation men experienced, in that way creating an exceptional text, inclusive of both men and women as capable of embracing the fullness of ascetic life, including practice and transformation, and of assisting others in the process.

That Palladius attributed value to acts of comparison and competition in the spiritual life may be demonstrated by examining his use of language of rivalry in the *History*. Comparison and competition, though admittedly not the same thing, work in symbiotic fashion in Palladius's text: recognition of differences between oneself and another created occasions for competitive behavior, either with the other or with the self whom one imagined one was no longer, or still hoped one might become. Palladius's past also shaped his understanding of how comparison and competition might be construed as positive tools in spiritual formation. That he was devoted to the apostle Paul, that he was a recognized Origenist[3] and a disciple of Evagrius Ponticus[4] disclose a variety of sources for his understanding of how interacting with others might prove educative and transformative for the ascetic. Third, close readings of three stories from *The Lausiac History* illustrate the nature of competitive behavior between desert daughters and desert sons and the devastation and transformation that result from such behavior.

3. Demetrios S. Katos, *Palladius of Helenopolis: The Origenist Advocate* (Oxford: Oxford University Press, 2011), 87.

4. Ibid., 13.

Early Christian Asceticism

It was inevitable that Christians in fourth-century Egypt notice one another. One of the initial impetuses to the movement to the desert and the thriving of ascetic life there was the fact that, due to a period of permissiveness granted Christianity by Constantine, religious practice grew lax. No longer was it necessary for an earnest Christian to endure martyrdom to prove his or her mettle; comparing one's aspirations to do so, even if the opportunity evaded one, meant looking rather askance at other Christians complacently accepting society's new tolerance. This constituted a judgment that ascetics made on the lives of less committed Christians, driving the more radical to places where their stricter ways of life were possible, because of the dissociation with and renouncing of social life that characterized life in the desert. The very background of early asceticism, then, is framed within a context of judgment and comparisons made between the lives of those remaining "in" the world and those who observed within themselves an ability and desire to perform more severe acts of piety and renunciation.

Georgia Frank illuminates the shift that happened in early Christian pilgrimages from sites linked to biblical events to sites where contemporary ascetic persons lived so that pilgrims might view how those lives indicated biblical, and thence Christian, reality. She writes that the mere face of the ascetic "constituted the meeting ground of the biblical past and the pilgrim's present. With a parallax vision capable of perceiving both ascetic achievement and biblical presence, the pilgrim could gaze at and through the face, a textured window onto the biblical past."[5] The importance of visual experience is demonstrated by a story of one of Antony's guests who, when asked after many visits why he did not ask the abba anything,

---

5. Georgia Frank, *The Memory of the Eyes: Pilgrims to Living Saints in Christian Late Antiquity* (Berkeley: University of California Press, 2000), 168.

replied: "It is enough for me to see you, Father" (Antony 27).
As Christian ascetics of fourth-century Egypt began to attract
attention for behavior increasingly foreign to "ordinary"
Christians, such as the famed Antony's entombing himself,[6]
which several ascetics, male and female alike, copy in Palladius's *History* (5.1; 45.2; 49.1), a consensus arose that the
less attached one was to human life, with its biological needs
of food, clothing, and shelter, the more privileged one's place
in a gradation of holiness reserved increasingly for practitioners
of asceticism. This "dying daily" of which both the apostle
Paul (1 Cor 15:31) and Antony spoke[7] was in deliberate
contrast to the lives many Christians believed were worth living. Palladius, too, appears fascinated by fantastic ascetic bodies and practices and, compared with the range of early
Christian literature on the subject, his examples are by no
means unusual. For instance, he describes one ascetic who had
"reached such a high degree of mortification and so wasted
away his body that the sun shone through his bones" (48.3).
Another applied a heated iron to his limbs whenever he felt
fleshly desire, until he "became ulcerated all over" (11.4).
Even Evagrius said, "I did not touch lettuce or any vegetable
greens, or fruit, or grapes, nor did I even take a bath, since
the time I came to the desert" (38.12). The severity of these
activities may have served to divert the attention of these
desert sons from their very real, natural, embodied needs.

Much of the early literature of monastic formation, however, diverts its focus from what an outsider might see and be
fascinated by to what the ascetic him- or herself experienced.
Such a focus necessarily had to deal with evaluation of the
other as recognizably "worse" than oneself, a comparison that
seems, if not justified, at least expected given the visitors from

6. Athanasius, *Life of Antony*, 37.
7. Ibid., 95.

cities with whom ascetics came into contact.[8] From the point of view of some desert daughters and desert sons, it would have been natural to see the obvious contrast between their behavior, acknowledged by both ascetics and audience alike to be more conducive to expressing committed Christian life, and that practiced by those believers remaining "in the world." As well, it is always easier to see flaws in others rather than those unrecognized in the self, so that when encounters with visitors resulted in recognition by the ascetic of the self as superior, a comparison and judgment had been made.

Though "worse" and "better" are generic terms, they indicate a gradation of values extant among early ascetics and their public to which Palladius himself adheres. In a brief account of two ascetics, Palladius advances three variations of what constitutes an ideal: living the "best life," progressing to the "highest love of God," and "practicing the perfect life" (61). Superlatives of this sort reinforce the notion that the type of life to which the ascetic desert daughter or desert son aspired was juxtaposed to lesser stages. The "high" or "highest" form of life to which one reached is repeatedly espoused by Palladius when he mentions "high degrees" of sanctity (57.1), self-control (59.1), and virtue (66.2) as benchmarks for his readers. Indeed, in the instance of the three qualities just named, it is significant that the latter two were attached to women and the first to a married couple, because such associations show that the asceticism by which one reached a superior "degree" of being was not relegated to just male or to just single, unmarried practitioners of asceticism. Palladius's vision of asceticism is inclusive, expansive, and illustrative of the variety of desert sons and desert daughters he met on his

---

8. That the "city" was not the abode of sinners only is evident, however, in a saying that relates a revelation to Antony that he had an "equal" in the city: "a doctor by profession and whatever he had beyond his needs he gave to the poor, and every day he sang the Sanctus with the angels" (Antony 24).

travels and of his understanding that each person's practices were chosen by a singular individual with a particular temperament and needs. Similarly, the "word" requested by desert sons and daughters from an elder was customized to the disciple's situation, resulting in his or her mulling over of the received word in order to change ascetic practice and experience transformation. Though we have already seen that this "word" should not be regarded as the sole locus of wisdom in the Christian desert tradition, meditation on and embodying such a word did function as ways by which desert sons and daughters could grow in their spiritual lives. And when such words "worked" in some effective manner, they were shared. As Thomas Merton writes,

> Those who came to the desert seeking "salvation" asked the elders for a "word" that would help them to find it—a *verbum salutis*, a "word of salvation." The answers were not intended to be general, universal prescriptions. Rather they were originally concrete and precise keys to particular doors that had to be entered, at a given time, by given individuals. Only later, after much repetition and much quotation, did they come to be regarded as common currency.[9]

In contrast to the "highest" sort of life to which the ascetic aspired was the cultivation of what might appear its opposite: humility. And, indeed, humility became a privileged monastic virtue. Because asceticism attracted the notice of so many in the Mediterranean cultures where it thrived in the first centuries of Christianity, one danger the ascetic always faced was being undermined by pride, for recognition by self and others of having attained to such a "high" state of life that the recognition obliterated the ascetic's continuing to live an authentic

9. Merton, *The Wisdom of the Desert: Sayings of the Desert Fathers of the Fourth Century* (Boston: Shambhala, 2004), 12–13.

Christian life. Stories abound in *The Sayings of the Desert Fathers and Mothers* warning disciples against letting pride get the better of them. The root of the problem was the presumption that should one compare oneself with another, one would inevitably regard oneself better. Even *The Lausiac History* tells of a virgin living in Jerusalem whose fall into sin is explained by her having thought better of herself than she ought to have done. The conclusion of her story states: "For as her thoughts were occupied in running down others, the guardian of her chastity was absent" (88). The linking of sexual sin with judgment, though an unlikely pairing, shows how dangerous it was for ascetics of either gender to be more vigilant about others' sins than their own.

In short, comparing oneself with others was prohibited in the practical advice of the desert elders, for it resulted in passing judgment which would endanger an ascetic's humility. Accordingly, refusing to assess the behavior of others, as either good or bad, demonstrated an accurate view of one's self, avowedly incapable in large part of controlling one's own thoughts as well as the body, though this in no way lessened the disciple's responsibility to do so. Discernment of thoughts created an opportunity for increased self-knowledge so that it became natural for the disciple to refrain from rendering judgment, knowing experientially that he or she was never in a position to judge. Matoes, for instance, explains the need to become aware of one's own faults, so that one set oneself below others (Matoes 11). To avoid casting aspersions on the behavior of others not only reflected the ascetic's true assessment of self but also resulted in a cessation of anxiety about the self, so that one desert son could say, "If you want to find rest here below, and hereafter, in all circumstances say, Who am I? and do not judge anyone" (Joseph of Panephysis 2). Another desert son rebutted temptations to think highly of himself by affirming an accurate assessment of himself, asking, "Am I to be compared with Abba Antony; am I become like

Abba Pambo, or like the other Fathers who pleased God?" (Isidore the Priest 6). Comparisons of oneself with established holy men reveal acute self-knowledge and, in effect, undermine the possibility of offering counsel to others, even to those "below" or "behind" one on the path to spiritual perfection, itself problematic. Though a trope, in some sense, used by countless monastics in subsequent centuries, admission of such humility did not ultimately dissuade a would-be disciple from pressing the elder for advice. If anything, it paradoxically reinforced the identity of such a one as the best person from whom advice might be sought.

Language of Rivalry

Language of rivalry is pervasive in *The Lausiac History* and derives from multiple sources. That Palladius deeply admired the apostle Paul is evident in repeated references to the Pauline letters and in his modeling his own journeys to visit desert daughters and sons on Paul's circulating among the first Christian churches. Palladius also inherited from Paul and the general context of protomonasticism a vocabulary of combat, linked to martyrdom, that might be used to describe spiritual warfare. Palladius extends this vocabulary, however, to describe not just the tempting thoughts against which the self fought, attached to Satan or demons, but also to describe how the ascetics he visited regarded one another as potential rivals, in some situations, that conditioned their competitive behavior, and to explain what exactly might be meant by such rivalry.

Palladius's admiration for Paul is shown by likening himself to the apostle in his framing of the *History*, both beginning and ending the work with reference to Paul, in addition to references throughout the work. In the Prologue, Palladius describes Paul as "so much his superior in way of life and in knowledge" (6), and like Paul, not content to merely hear reports of virtue, Palladius travels to meet the desert Christians (ibid.). Palladius even amplifies his own motivation to make his travels, in contrast to Paul's desire for first-hand experience, by saying that he journeyed and wrote of the ascetics' lives "not so much to do them a good turn as to help myself!" (ibid.). Paul's terminology of spiritual warfare as reminiscent of the martyr's arena is adopted by Palladius as well. The foreword to *The Lausiac History* is peppered with references to "unconquered athletes" (3) and "athletes of Christ, men and women" (5), whose "contests in the arena" (4) and "in the arena of piety" (5) Palladius recorded.

Similarly, the final chapter of *The Lausiac History* contains reference to Paul as Palladius says of himself (in the third person), "He is satisfied with what he has at hand; he is even thankful if despised" (71.1) echoing Paul's Philippians 4:11 and 1 Thessalonians 5:18, respectively; further, Palladius says, "For such an one I will glory" quoting Paul directly (71.4). His technique in the last chapter of referring to himself in the third person is taken from Paul (2 Cor 12:2-5), the chapter functioning as a cryptic description of Palladius himself, whom he calls "the brother who has been with me from youth until this very day" (71.1). This distancing of himself from himself, in order to avoid deliberate solicitation of admiration, also reinforces the conclusion to which his work has been drawing. It is not merely the other against whom one competes; it is against the version of oneself pitted against that other which falls short that one finally competes.

But it was not just from Pauline theology that Palladius inherited his use of language of combat associated with Christian asceticism and spiritual progress. In the early third-century *Martyrdom of Saints Perpetua and Felicitas*, for instance, Perpetua describes a vision she had, saying: "At the foot of the ladder lay a dragon of enormous size, and it would attack those who tried to climb up and try to terrify them from doing so. . . . Slowly, as though he were afraid of me, the dragon stuck his head out from underneath the ladder. Then, using it as my first step, I trod on his head and went up."[10] It is significant that Perpetua envisages how the "head" of the beast might prove part of the ladder by which she ascends to "higher" life, in that such an incorporation of the ordeal by which her death was effected provides a clear picture of the way that asceticism—fighting the temptations of both body and mind—appropriated this sort of metaphor. Later, the account also records that against the women a mad heifer had been chosen "that their [the young women's] sex might be matched with that of the beast."[11] The practice of matching competitors well is also used by Origen, though in a different context. His father having been martyred in 201, Origen's use of imagery of the contests in *On First Principles* is especially poignant. He writes that

> just as those who preside over the games do not allow the competitors to oppose one another indiscriminately or by chance in the contests, but after a careful examination match them in equal pairs according to size and years, this one with that . . . so also must we understand in regard to the divine providence, that it treats all who descend into the struggles of human life with the most impartial care, according to the nature of each individual's virtue, which [God] alone knows.[12]

Thus, "in the eyes of God, each particular human spirit had been allotted a particular physical constitution as its appropriate sparring partner. Each person's flesh and blood was particular to that person, and had been exquisitely calibrated by God . . . to challenge the potentially mighty spirit of each to

10. "The Martyrdom of Saints Perpetua and Felicitas" in *The Acts of the Christian Martyrs*, trans. Herbert Musurillo (Oxford: Clarendon Press, 1972), 111.

11. Ibid., 129.

12. Origen, *On First Principles*, trans. G. W. Butterworth (New York: Harper & Row, 1966), 215.

stretch beyond itself."[13] Origen's understanding of Christian asceticism, then, is that each person is equipped with his or her own struggles that are perfectly mediated and fought by the flesh. Evagrius uses similar battle imagery, associating tempting thoughts—*logismoi*—with the demonic: "Wrestlers are not the only ones whose occupation it is to throw others down and to be thrown in turn; the demons too wrestle—with us. Sometimes they throw us and at other times it is we who throw them."[14] The desert tradition is full of allusions to battling temptation in the language of the arena: Syncletica, for instance, says "Those who are great athletes must contend against stronger enemies" (Syncletica 14).

Metaphorical descendants of the martyrs in the arenas, desert daughters and sons carried on the battles with tempting thoughts—Evagrius's *logismoi*—and Palladius, too, is deliberate about his use of "contest" and "arena" when reporting, "I went to the contests in the arena" (4) and "I have recorded only a few of their lesser contests" (5) to describe what he saw. Yet the language extends beyond the demons to whom the passionate thoughts were attached by Evagrius and begins to sound very much as if it were a matter of contending with one's fellow. This happens in two stages. First, Palladius designates the enemies of two of his heroine ascetics, Melania the Elder and Melania the Younger, as "beasts" (54.5) and "the mouth of the lion" (61.5). The people so identified are members of Roman society who opposed the women's giving away of property, acts that likely countered the sensibilities of those for whom civilization and ownership of property and goods defined culture and its stabilization. But it is interesting that Palladius even places the two women in some relation to one another, saying of the Younger that her virtue "excelled that of even elderly women

---

13. Peter Brown, *The Body and Society: Men, Women, and Sexual Renunciation in Early Christianity* (New York: Columbia University Press, 1988), 165.
14. Evagrius, *Praktikos*, 35.

far advanced in holiness" (61.1), possibly including her grand-mother. Further, Melania the Younger was "continually stung by the stories about her grandmother [Melania the Elder]" (ibid.) to such an extent that she wanted to emulate her and ended up "excelling" even as a young woman over those who were her seniors.

This is fairly tame language of comparison and competition, but Palladius goes further, recording deliberate attempts by ascetics to rival others. After Pior's death, for instance, "a good many monks strove to rival him by staying in his cell, but they could not finish out a year, for the place [was] terrible and without one redeeming feature" (39.3). Another's asceticism was so severe that "no one dared to rival him" (43.1). Further, Palladius reports of this desert son, "Because of his excessive self-control and all-night vigils he was actually suspected of being a monster" (ibid.). The extremity of this ascetic's prac-tice established him even beyond human nature, so that his asceticism, central to his identity, made him a terror to his neighbors. But Palladius does not limit such feats to men. As his advice to Lausus states that both holy men and women enable revelations concerning the state of one's own heart, so Palladius notes that he "must also commemorate in this book the courageous women whom God granted struggles equal to those of men, so that no one could plead as an excuse that women are too weak to practice virtue successfully" (41.1). It is, in fact, in his stories that include both men and women in conversation and confrontation that revelation of character happens most explicitly, so that not just men are edified by the presence of stalwart women in the desert alongside them-selves but that women, too, seem to have been made aware of their own authentic condition in relation to others, self, and God through their interactions with men.

Just as attention was given to the experience of judging others, accounting them worse than oneself, so less attention was given in the literature of the Christian desert tradition to the opposite experience. What happened when desert daughters and desert sons made the acquaintance of others more advanced on the spiritual path than themselves? This happened regularly when establishing relations with a recognized elder and must, too, have been the case for Palladius himself and for his readers bent on growing spiritually by reading tales of men and women holier than themselves. For them, Palladius built into his *History* a series of stories that affirmed comparing, at least when it led to self-betterment and not despair. Demetrios S. Katos writes that

> Although [Palladius] had addressed his work to Lausus, he also wrote with an eye towards the whole imperial court, which at the time was ruled by the powerful older sister of Theodosius II, Aelia Pulcheria. . . . Her political power was cresting just as Palladius addressed his work to Lausus in 420, and she (whom Lausus may have served personally) was certainly one of his intended readers.[15]

Palladius's intention is explicit in the prologue: "Seek for meetings with holy men and women so that you may see clearly your own hearts. . . . The comparison will enable you to see your own sluggishness" (15). Further, having seen one's own sluggishness, Palladius believes change is possible. Even among aristocratic readers, situated in environments much different than most of what is described in the *History*, edification might occur. For just as the desert son Antony of Egypt was told of an individual more advanced than he, living a secular life in the city, demonstrates that no one was immune from the possibility of being shown up by another "better" than oneself, so aristocrats might consider their own unique circumstances which permitted their reading Palladius's text as capable of occasioning their own transformation. Though

15. Katos, *Palladius*, 104–5.

Antony's reaction to another's superiority was not recorded, the fact that the story circulated meant that it in no way impaired the prestige with which Antony was regarded. It was, in fact, confirmation of his very humanness—it being only human to discover that, in relation to others, one always has more to learn.

Inferiority as a Positive Good: Three Stories

In *The Lausiac History*, accounts of confrontation between female and male ascetics usually make use of gender as a means to deepen the impact of the male ascetics' surprise over the valor and accomplishment of women. Though this may be unsettling to some degree—gender being relegated to a mere tool—it is hard to overlook the unique character of Palladius's attitude toward women in general. He was, after all, an open admirer of the famed Melania the Elder, devoting two chapters to her (46, 54) and highlighting her key role in Evagrius's conversion to monastic life (38.8-9). That the women in the stories considered below were not mere props, intended to reveal opportunities for men to be transformed, is emphasized by the inclusion, in two of them, of the women's own epiphanies that rate as experiences just as profound as the men's.

Each of the stories includes reference to specific ascetic activities, including prayer practices, dietary restrictions, and renunciation of social ties and interaction. Each story also explores the ramifications of renouncing particular ideas of the self in order to mature spiritually. In this way, Palladius deconstructs expectations for what constitutes "ideal" ascetic behavior, locating it not exclusively in diet or prayer or seclusion, but expecting his reader to note which stories within the whole of his text most particularly speak to the reader's heart. The stories examined below fall into categories of experience of challenge and defeat, self-acceptance, and self-criticism.

Challenge and Defeat

Palladius seems particularly to have enjoyed finding ascetics whose roving lifestyles he might approve, being prone to wandering himself. This was the case with Sarapion, a desert son who was proficient at asceticism, but who could not remain in the cell—in addition to humility, another supreme monastic virtue, as another desert son famously declared "your cell will teach you everything" (Moses 6). Palladius excuses this "fault" in Sarapion by concluding his introduction of him, "It was not that he was distracted by material things; he wandered about the world and successfully perfected this virtue, for that was his nature. For there are differences in natures, but not in substance" (37.1). This commonality of substance is important when we consider our gendered belonging; one with the human family, we yet each express an individual nature to which we must be faithful. Palladius seems cognizant of this distinction when excusing Sarapion's behavior that seems to deviate from behavior emerging as normative for the desert sons and daughters. Palladius evidently sees no point in blaming Sarapion for his inability to stay in the cell, perhaps because he, too, was unable to remain long in one place.

Having ventured to Rome in his travels, Sarapion is told of a particularly worthy virgin in the city and he visits her. She had, apparently, remained enclosed in her dwelling for twenty-five years (37.14), and the story seems to hint at Sarapion's having picked up on some kind of arrogance in her about that fact that provokes his challenge of her leaving her home. She does, in fact, take up his challenge and goes to church, but this is not enough for Sarapion. He provokes her further, the question revolving around how thoroughly dead to the opinions of others this desert daughter had become. Sarapion tells her "[I]f you wish really to convince me you are dead and no longer alive, pleasing men, do as I do and I will know that you are dead. Disrobe yourself and place your clothing on your shoulders and go through the middle of the city with me in the lead in this way" (37.15). The maiden resists, thinking such an action would scandalize others and the terms in which her objection arises are telling: others would think her "insane and demon-ridden" (ibid.). It is arguable that Sarapion's challenge is an offense to her and others' modesty, but Sarapion seems to think she is equivocating. "And so far as you are concerned," he asks, "what does it matter?" (ibid.). At this point, she stands her ground, claiming she will do anything else he asks, but not this, and Palladius reports believing that she was humbled and her pride broken by this encounter (37.16).

In this story, the reaction to news of an ascetic more advanced than himself resulted in Sarapion's needing to validate the news by seeing for himself. His ability to see through what others thought exemplary and to offer a challenge to the virgin seems to underscore his superiority; not only is he able to operate in ways that challenge Roman society—parading the streets naked—but he is also able to see through its most cherished notions of what constituted exemplary behavior: a virgin remaining sequestered in her home for twenty-five years. Sarapion goes to the heart of the problem, confronting the virgin herself and providing the means by which she is made aware of the fallibility of her own idea of herself as dead to the world. Rather than just leaving her humbled and broken, Sarapion offered her an opportunity to revision herself and to grow in a way more consistent with the way of Christian life she had adopted and the seclusion under which she lived.

Self-Acceptance

In another story, the ascetic life of Piteroum, called "Saint" and "the famous anchorite" by Palladius (34.3), is interrupted by a visit from an angel who chides him for thinking well of himself for his piety and residing alone (34.3). As in the conversation between Sarapion and the virgin in Rome, when the two compare notes about what is meant by "journeying to

God" (37.13) and whether such a journey entails movement in the flesh or spirit, Palladius's motivation in Piteroum's story seems to be to dismantle the assumption that eremitical life is superior to cenobitic. Much earlier in his text, he had advanced this notion when reporting the appeal of a community of desert sons to the famous desert father, Pambo, when a "rivalry developed among the brethren" (14.4) in regard to two deceased brothers whose ascetic lives had varied considerably. Pambo insists, "Both were perfect. One showed the work of Abraham; the other, that of Elias" (ibid.). In this way, Palladius showed rivalry between action (represented by Abraham's hospitality) and contemplation (represented by Elias's seclusion in the wilderness) as inappropriate. The angelic visitor challenges Piteroum: "Why do you think so much of yourself for being pious and residing in a place such as this?" (34.3). Further, the angel asks, "Do you want to see someone more pious than yourself, a woman? . . . She is better than you are" (ibid). As in the case of Sarapion, it is not enough for Piteroum to be told of the woman's existence, he, too, must verify with his eyes what he has heard with his ears. He travels to the woman's community, is admitted on account of his age and reputation (34.4), and reveals the status of its lowliest server, a woman[16] who has been feigning madness—its own curious element in the story that allows Palladius to play with the juxtaposition of wisdom and folly described by the apostle Paul (1 Cor 3:18)—by calling her *amma*, a revelation that unwittingly disrupts the internal dynamics of the community in two ways. First, the other women are aghast at having formerly treated the seemingly insignificant woman in so slovenly

16. Known as Isidora the Fool, this "nun who feigned madness" is recognized as a saint by both the Roman Catholic and Eastern Orthodox Churches, with her feast day falling on May 1. See Michael Walsh, *A New Dictionary of Saints: East and West* (Collegeville, MN: Liturgical Press, 2007), 285.

a manner (34.7), and, second, the lowly woman, unable to bear the accolades of Piteroum and the community, abandons the community.

Piteroum's reaction to the woman, however, is held up as a model. When the angel appears and accurately diagnoses his problem, "you dwell here and wander about cities in your mind" (34.4), he, too, like the unnamed Roman virgin, is willing to leave his dwelling—in her case for the first time in twenty-five years, but in Piteroum's case for the first time ever—at least, as far as the text reveals, calling Piteroum, "he who had never gone away" (34.4). Piteroum is also not moved by the appearance of other worthy women in the community who might have been the one mentioned by the angel. He displays penetrating insight into the character of God in recognizing that it would only be the lowliest in the community who is most honored by God. Finding her, Piteroum says, "I pray that I may be deemed as worthy as she on the Day of Judgment" (34.6), revealing in her status as desert daughter an authoritative stature conditioned by many years of service. Rather than take the angel's words as a reason to confirm his own complacency, Piteroum is willing to be challenged, and his humility in the face of another's superiority results in his achieving greater knowledge of himself. Seeming satisfied with himself before the angel's visit, he is open to truth of himself which he could not have manufactured himself. Although Palladius elsewhere upholds the centrality of conscience—speaking of Didymus the Blind, for instance, as one who "had an excellent natural teacher—his own conscience" (4.2)—Piteroum needed the angel's word to move him out of himself and engage him with the possibility of others who might model true holiness to him. Witnessing such an exemplar, he is willing to see the value of communal life in contrast to his own, in that communal life afforded this woman opportunities to imitate Christ. It is worthwhile being cautious about this value, however, in that we can see that it virtually mandates a life of servitude of some to others, in this case a woman to other women. This kind of story would best serve the interests of those in positions of power (usually men) able to persuade others without power that their powerlessness makes uniquely possible a life of imitating Christ for which they should be grateful.

Whereas earlier in his text, Palladius affirmed the equality of active and contemplative modes of Christian life in the words of Pambo, here he seizes an opportunity to dismantle any superiority built into the eremitical life by juxtaposing it with the cenobitic. Just as the literature of the Christian desert tradition affirmed the opportunities for transformation at the hands of the other by uncovering the fallacy of trying to avoid people in order to avoid sin[17] or by rhetorically asking the solitary whose feet he washed,[18] so Palladius adds his voice: neither vocation is superior to the other. Against the tendency to privilege the solitary life, Palladius does his best to restore the balance, so as to build into his program of mutual edification an articulation of the value of the "other" in order that his reader not forget an important function of his or her reading. Palladius's voice may be heard echoing with the angel's, reminding the reader, especially Lausus and his friends, members of the royal court obviously in social contact with others: you might envy those with the temperament and inclination

17. Helen Waddell, trans., *The Desert Fathers* (New York: Vintage Books, 1998), 94–95. Saying 33 describes an unnamed brother living in community whose anger drives him to solitude where he finds other opportunities to vent his feelings (against inanimate objects), the moral of the story being to highlight the fallacy of thinking that removal from the company of others will dispel temptation to sin.

18. Basil, "The Long Rules," in *Ascetical Works*, trans. M. Monica Wagner, Fathers of the Church 9 (Washington, DC: Catholic University of America Press, 1962), 252.

to live alone, but consider the value of your own place in life and make the best of it.

The "mad nun" in the story is changed as well. Having previously served the community incognito, she is distressed by an outsider's applauding her and enlisting others in the community to honor her. She seems to have had a certain sure sense of herself before Piteroum's arrival that revolved around her assumption of the role of the community's fool. After the revelation of herself and recognition of herself by others, she cannot maintain her past identity, which has been thoroughly destabilized by Piteroum. Her sense of self seems to have been founded on her remaining unrecognized, and her wisdom in knowing how to deal with its upset had profound consequences for herself and her community. It is worthwhile noting, as well, how Piteroum's revelation of her situation resulted in her deciding no longer to be complicit in a system that oppressed her. Her leaving the community could be interpreted as not only an intolerance of the accolades she was receiving for her humility, but also an intolerance to maintain the dualistic status quo of oppressor/oppressed, profane/holy, or rational/mad—even when these pairings seem to be challenged and even reversed by Piteroum's engagement with the community. Her disappearance tears a hole in the social fabric woven around the dysfunctional relationships the community members had created. Significantly, Palladius notes that nobody knew where she went or how she died (34.7); in a sense, she disappears into the text, the indeterminacy of her end acting as a kind of signal to the reader that the place where one's following of Christ leads one, and the transformations that ensue, are largely unknown beforehand. The disruptions to the woman's life, as in the case of the Roman virgin, are severe enough to result in a thorough dismantling of her whole established mode of being, and an invitation to the work of dismantling systemic injustice we remain a part of in our own day.

Self-Criticism

In a final story about a desert son named Paul, an actual meeting with an exemplary desert daughter is not detailed. Instead, the mere report of a woman's ascetic practices was enough to dismay him. He hastens to Macarius to confess:

> I am dejected. . . . In a certain village there lives a virgin who has practiced asceticism for thirty years. They say that she eats nothing except on Saturday and Sunday. But in the whole period of five days she spends between eating, she says seven hundred prayers. And I felt sorry for myself when I learned of that, because I cannot say more than three hundred. (20.2)

This report is worth relating in full for two reasons. First, it conveys a specific program of asceticism, including details of diet, prayer, and longevity of praxis and, second, it explicitly expresses what about the woman's regimen caused Paul's distress: the number of prayers the woman regularly prayed compared to the number he managed seems to have undermined his sense of his own value. Though his appeal to Macarius is not specific, it results in Macarius's well-balanced reply. Like many spiritual elders of the desert, Macarius offers advice through the prism of his own experience and it is specifically crafted to meet the needs of the one who hears it. First, Macarius is open about his own practice as it edifies Paul, admitting that it takes him a full week, not just five weekdays as in the case of the woman, to accomplish seven hundred prayers, and he does other things besides, supporting himself and making time to counsel others (20.3). Second, he highlights reason as the means by which to determine whether information about another person's behavior should distress him, saying "my reason tells me that I am not negligent" (ibid.). He reasons that God is content with his practice and tells Paul that "if you say three hundred prayers and your reason bothers you, it is clear that you do not say them with simplicity of heart, or else you could say more and do not" (ibid.).

In addition to providing Paul with sensible advice, Macarius the Alexandrian also has a chapter in the *History* devoted to himself in which it is interesting to note the variety of practices that this same Macarius found his reason telling him he ought to try during different phases of his own ascetic career. "Such was his practice," reports Palladius, "that whenever he heard of any asceticism, he surpassed it to perfection" (18.1). He tried going without cooked food, he tried eating only raw vegetables for seven years, and he went through a period of measuring his bread consumption by what his hand, acting as "toll-collector," might draw out through the "narrow neck" of a jar (20.1-2). All of these dietary decisions were made because of reports that Macarius had heard of some other person's practice in a clear attempt to rival what others were doing. Further, he himself proved a challenge to a Pachomian community that he entered incognito and was eventually compelled to leave for having shamed the brothers with his superhuman asceticism, about which the brothers complained to their superior, "Where did you get this bodiless man for our condemnation?" (18.15). The community's leader showed remarkable wisdom in approaching Macarius gently, saying, "I am grateful to you for having made my children knuckle down so that they might not become haughty about their own ascetic practices" (18.16), but then he requests that Macarius leave. In this story, Palladius shows the reader that ascetics are human, too. They indulge in typical responses to realizing that another person is capable of accomplishing more than oneself: anger, quarreling, and criticism directed at another rather than oneself.

In contrast, Macarius's advice to the worried Paul was to temper his expectations of himself with what God expected of him. Clearly the report of the woman's abilities revealed what he felt was the paltry nature of his own abilities compared to his expectations of himself, but this revelation issued in a possibility of transformation. Though it feels a bit too contemporary to deem Macarius's advice a simple "accept yourself," there is something ancient in its corollary of "know thyself" espoused by Greek philosophers and by Origen,[19] who had a profound influence on Evagrius, and thence on Palladius. But not only is knowledge of oneself necessary, but knowledge of the event and what has happened enables a person to understand the self better: Why did Paul react in this way? As one desert son said (and this is a saying important enough for me to have selected it as this text's epigraph), "Not understanding what has happened prevents us from going on to something better" (Poemen 200), and this shows very well the significance of stopping to pay attention to what about a situation has bothered a person and how one's interacting in the situation either reveals something about one's tendencies or even uncovers things about oneself that previously was unknown, in order that by reflecting on them they become known. Palladius was aware of the importance of acquiring knowledge, of others and oneself, in the process of maturing spiritually. In the case of Paul's story, the moral of the story could be that one's truest rival is oneself, emphasized by the failure of the rival actually to appear in the story itself. But it is important to point out that Paul did not, possibly could not, have reached this conclusion by himself. He needed the sounding board of another against whom he might admit distress and acknowledge his weakness, and then from whom to receive advice. This sort of relationship and exchange seems an incipient form of institutionalized confession or spiritual direction, where space is made between the self and other, in which one's true self may be

19. See Origen's *Commentary on the Song of Songs* 2.5, where he says, "It seems to me, that the soul ought to acquire self-knowledge of a twofold kind: she should know both what she is in herself, and how she is actuated; that is to say, she ought to know what she is like essentially, and what she is like according to her dispositions."

acknowledged through admission of distressing emotions and the encouragement to look deeply into what truly is the source of one's weakness.

In all of these stories, another person was necessary for revelation of character to occur. Emphases on solitude in the desert and stability in the cell found in the literature of the Christian desert tradition must be balanced with advice sought from a wise elder. In addition to exchanges with a recognized elder, there were also many occasions when coming into contact with other desert daughters and sons with whom one was learning resulted in lessons learned. Even the rumor of an accomplished person, in the case of Paul, could result in self-revelation, opening up the possibility that the text of *The Lausiac History* itself might occasion its readers' transformation. Thus Palladius framed his work, expecting readers to find the act of reading a discipline itself that enabled discovery of others likely to help one in one's own spiritual maturing. Further, Palladius's description of a wide range of ascetic behaviors seems deliberately constructed in order to include something for everyone. That his fascination with food proves self-implicating of his own weakness reveals a human tendency to give particular attention to those things of relevance to oneself. Indeed, nowhere is Palladius's account of himself quite so endearing in the *History* as when he allays his intimidation in the presence of the great John of Lycopolis. Palladius responds to John's question about his desire to become bishop by joking that he already was a bishop. John asks about his jurisdiction and Palladius replies:

> In the kitchen and shops, over the tables and pots. I examine them, and if there is any sour wine I excommunicate it, but I drink the good. Likewise I inspect the pots, too, and if any salt or other spices are lacking, I throw these in and thus season them and eat them. This is my diocese, for Gluttony has ordained me for her child. (35.10)

John of Lycopolis is not offended by Palladius's irreverence
and confirms that Palladius will one day be bishop. As such,
he must have interacted widely with members of the church,
clergy and laity, and realized the effectiveness of literature
devoted to edifying its readers. Thus his own intent to edify
enabled his crafting a significant contribution to Christian
literature, which is also a profound testament for readers in
the twenty-first century of how spiritual progress operates in
practical, everyday associations between believers committed
to their calling. That Palladius took seriously a very real element of human life is evident in his offering a nuanced view
of how comparison and competition might aid a believer's
forming a more accurate picture of him- or herself and chang-
ing for the better. As Jay Newman argues,

> Religious competition is not itself a problem; but unless we
> understand it and fully appreciate its importance in social
> life, we shall have only a cloudy and incomplete vision of
> the sources of destructive religious conflict. Destructive
> religious conflict is often the result of religious competition
> having gone awry, and those who would fight against reli-
> gious violence and persecution must reflect on how religious
> competition can be regulated so that it will result in spiritual
> progress rather than misery and despair.[20]

Though seemingly "perfect" men and women were depicted
in the literature of the Christian desert tradition, their portraits
were idealized and the typical encounter that a person had,
and continues to have, with others is with people at various
points in their spiritual maturing. Early literature would have
its readers believe that attainment of perfection, of the best
sort of life or the highest sort of life (all terms which Palladius

---

20. Jay Newman, *Competition in Religious Life* (Ontario: Wilfrid Laurier
University Press, 1989), 214.

uses interchangeably), is possible if one only travels long enough, but human experience offers an important reminder that there are always others accompanying on the way, offering us a helping hand over troubling terrain or reaching to us for help. And others accompany us with whom we merely and gratefully join hands for love.

CHAPTER FIVE

The Way of Love in the Christian Desert

In this book, women's persistence in the desert tradition when they were not wanted there has been implicitly characterized as love. Sometimes these women have called out these men in word or deed, occasioning further examination of their ways of life. For instance, Ammonas feigned madness when some people came to him, appealing for his judgment on a matter (Ammonas 9). A woman observing the interaction names Ammonas's folly and apparently Ammonas heard her words, though spoken to a neighbor and not directly to Ammonas, and he lamented his exposure. This is, in fact, a puzzling story because you would think on the face of it that this woman was confirming Ammonas's inability to judge, helping to release him from an obligation he seems to want to avoid. He could have gone along with her words, not heeding them, and continued to act the fool. Instead, he calls attention to them and rebukes her for occasioning his loss of something it had taken him many years to acquire. The story seems to play on contrasts between wisdom and folly, truth and deception, men's humility and women's outspokenness in public spaces. Whatever the intention between the interaction between Ammonas and the woman, the story implies that

Ammonas has been exposed and will now take up the duty of serving in judgment. Woman has been used here to circumvent the humility men were supposed to adopt; woman has been used here to allow a man to regain his position of superiority. Stories of this kind continue to puzzle and frustrate the contemporary reader for what they seem to suggest of holiness, the spiritual life, and public engagement.

The Troubling Aspect of Men's Love

A way of life could be surmised from men's interactions with one another. Their persistent presence to one another is also part of the Christian desert tradition. However, it seems to operate in ways that reinforce the patriarchal, hierarchical structure of relationships and community within the Christian desert. For instance, one story that is paradigmatic of desert obedience tells of a disciple Mark whose "master" is Silvanus. This story begins with the clarification of their relationship in this way: "The old man [Silvanus] loved him because of his obedience" (Mark 1). Other disciples of Silvanus were jealous of this relationship and, numbered at eleven, they are certain to recall to our minds the disciples of Jesus and tribes of Israel. In both cases of biblical communities, preferential treatment was evident in the "beloved" disciple and in Joseph, Jacob's favored son whom Rachel bore. When other elders in the desert story observe the dysfunction in the community occasioned by this jealousy, they "reproach" Silvanus for it. Rather than take their words to heart, however, Silvanus decides to illustrate just how obedient, and thus worthy of love, Mark is, especially in contrast to the other eleven disciples. He calls each and the only one who comes immediately when called is Mark. Indeed, Silvanus takes the elders into Mark's cell and exhibits how Mark's obedience had been so prompt he had not even finished writing a letter he had begun writing. The elders are converted and affirm that they, too, love Mark and know that God loves him, too.

This story is obviously meant to demonstrate the exemplary quality of obedience and to confirm further community members in their own resolve to be obedient to their own "masters." That this saying refers repeatedly to *love*, however, as it makes this point regarding the value of obedience, is troubling in that it equates one's worthiness for love with obedience and suggests that the only way one may experience love within the master-disciple relationship is by way of obedience. One must do something in particular to earn another's love.

Similarly, the next saying documents another occasion when Silvanus wished to demonstrate Mark's obedience and to justify his own love for Mark.

> They said this of Abba Silvanus that, as he was walking to Scetis one day with the old men and, wishing to demonstrate his disciple Mark's obedience, and show the reason for his affection for him, he said to him, seeing a small wild boar, 'Boy, do you see that little buffalo?' He said to him, 'Yes, abba.' 'And do you see his horns, how attractive they are?' He said to him, 'Yes, abba.' The old men were astonished at his reply and edified by his obedience. (Mark 2)

The efficacy of this interaction relies on Mark's willingness to not correct an error in identifying the local fauna that his master has likely made intentionally. Rather, Mark is complicit with Silvanus and the rest of the male company he is keeping by accepting and affirming the errors of their judgment. This constitutes a marvelous kind of love that the other men might rightly approve of, given the implications it has for confirming their own values and way of life in the desert.

These two stories about Mark are the first of a total of five under his name in the Alphabetical Collection, and each story represents Mark as a man for whom we might feel sorry. He has wholly resigned himself to the desert relationship with Silvanus that was held up as an example for others and the affection they seem to share is admired by others. And yet the next two stories about him recall his mother to the scene. In the first she attempts to visit him, and when Mark is in her presence, he closes his eyes, calling out greetings, and is dressed in such ragged garments that his mother does not even recognize him. When she goes to Silvanus and requests another audience with her son, Silvanus then goes to Mark and asks him to again appear before his mother. Obedience again enters the conversation as, apparently, Mark is reluctant to interact with his mother and yet does not want to disobey Silvanus if instructed to meet his mother; he thus pleads with Silvanus not to give him such orders and Silvanus does not. In a way, this may offer some relief to the reader loathe to think of Silvanus just ordering Mark around willy-nilly, manipulating him, without being sensitive to Mark's own needs.

Instead then of complying with Mark's mother's wishes, Silvanus tells her she has seen her son, even if she had not recognized him. The story ends as Silvanus comforts Mark's mother and sends her away. What her feelings are at this point are only implied in her being represented as the object of Silvanus's act of comforting. But if she felt anger or sadness, we likely would not be surprised. Mark's having to close his eyes when seeing her recalls similar strategies on the part of the desert sons to avoid making memories of women, whether family members or not, that might trouble them on their own time. It also suggests a vulnerability in Mark—that if he were to see his mother, to note her eagerness to see him or even recall him to the family life he might still have been able to enjoy—that he is anxious to resist.

The fourth story in the collection of stories associated with Mark refers to his decision to leave Scetis and live at Mount Sinai. We may wonder at this opening that he had the freedom to make such a decision and to wonder, further, what might have occasioned it. Could the master and disciple have had a falling out? Could jealousies among the disciples of Silvanus have finally alienated Mark so that he wanted to leave? If our spirits rise at all at this show of independence, they are quickly crushed when the story continues. His mother sends him a message, begging to see him "with tears" (Mark 4) and Silvanus orders him to go. At this, Mark beginning to obey by collecting all he needs to begin his journey, "bursts into tears and did not go after all." Surprisingly, he seems to have disobeyed Silvanus's order by not going. But we also learn that by "not going" he will not be moving to Mount Sinai after all and will remain in Scetis with Silvanus. Again, like in the case mentioned much earlier in this book when Poemen "took possession" of the man who had been married and had a child, this relationship may have, to contemporary ears, an ominous quality. The final story perhaps bears this out. When Silvanus decides to go to Syria, Mark cannot stand to be left alone without him and begs him to stick around for at least three days and in those three days, Mark dies. Rather than lose his relationship with this man who seems to have taken possession of him, he dies.

In terms of intimate and strong relationships with others, these stories about Mark may be attractive in detailing the possibilities for security and guidance that some desert sons may have needed when they left their families and decided against forming families of their own. However, there is also a mysteriously ominous quality attendant upon descriptions of such relationships, as if these ostensibly younger men substituted a wise elder guru for their relationship with God and family and relied wholly upon this other, older man for subsistence. In this particular series of five stories, we find this interdependent relationship characterized as love and affection which we may or may not want to accept as a valid form of creating or expressing love.

Men with Hearts of Stone

Poemen has been a consistent male figure to engage from the desert literature in this book as he has so many stories and sayings attributed to him. In this section I want to review two stories that detail Poemen's interactions with female family members. The first has to do with his mother, and it resembles in large degree the same kind of resistance that Mark showed above in meeting with his mother. Living with other men, both Mark and Poemen do not want to interact with their mothers. Poemen seems, however, to be living also with blood relations for whom his mother is also their mother. Rather than Mark's subservience to Silvanus that usurps any respect he might have shown his visiting mother, Poemen seems to assume responsibility for the men of his compound and works to keep the older female figure remote from them. He does this first by engaging her in conversation from the inside of the gate which has been shut in her face, so that ostensibly they cannot see one another but their voices meet across the barrier. In fact, not only does the mother's spoken desire to see her sons meet Poemen's ears but her weeping and wailing at being denied such affectionate presence meets his ears. His inquiring into her distress, as if he has no idea why she might be troubled, heightens her distress and she asks some really pointed questions: "What does it matter if I see you? Am I not your mother? Did I not nurse you?" (Self-Control 40).

This is a distressing story for readers when we consider the appalling neglect this mother experienced when legitimately desiring to visit her sons. That the brothers shut the gate in her face does not seem intended to cause us repugnance; rather, this is evidence of the men's firm stance toward distancing themselves quite literally from ties with family (especially female) members. That Poemen is considered to be merciless when engaging his mother in conversation through the gate is represented as exemplary, whereas his mother's grief and emotional outburst is represented as excessive. Just the fact that the brothers refuse to interact with their mother should strike us as evidence of the kind of spiritual life these men were creating on their own, one that required this kind of treatment of their mother. This is the same man, if we take the stories about Poemen to be about a single person, who when he saw a brother dozing in the assembly would not wake or rebuke the brother but put the brother's head on his knees and let him rest (Poemen 92). Perhaps this apparent discrepancy in his character would surprise us were we not aware of, and consistently made aware of, the firm line the sayings are drawing between the biological family and the faith community family, the second being privileged. Indeed, one has to wonder at the specifically gendered nature of this rejection of family members, for Poemen is among brothers, literally. These are men who were birthed from this common mother, and yet their rejection of family members does not extend to one another. Rather, Poemen's insistence on his mother's going away from the gate of their compound may have been doubly reinforced because of his brothers' presence with him. He was not only safeguarding his own well-being but could pride himself on safeguarding those of the men with whom he lived: a virtue within this tradition, indeed.

Another point to be made about this story is how easily the mother is pacified by a reminder that she *will* see her sons again in the future life and that this reality is contingent somehow on her not seeing them now. She is offered, indeed, a great power: in refusing to see her sons now, she safeguards their fallibility in memory of the female form and its destructive potential in their imagination and succumbing to sexual temptation through act. As we saw in the story about the son regarding his mother's body as fire, from which (if touched) would come the memory of other women's bodies and that this memory would remain with him, scorched in his mind and heart, we see here the woman as complicit with this mindset—sent away, even with joy, eager to participate in the drama enfolding her sons that would cause them to refuse her. We may even see her making a false move in her initial attempt to make contact with them, by pointing out her agedness, her "white hair," but recalling along with this her identity as one who suckled her sons. Having nursed them, she imagines she has pride of place in their world, and so she should. And, yet, this reminder is a false step in evoking the feminine more generally as that which is generative and fecund and nurturing, in body and gesture. This memory is what her sons must avoid at all costs—including refusing to see their mother. She is sent away with joy, having been convinced that her action of accepting their refusal to see her certifies her future seeing them again. This has to be what imminent readers of this literature thought for themselves: that they hoped family members would, like this mother, be complicit in their own denial of family connections, both those of their origin and those they might create as adults, and go away with joy or not approach at all, to begin with.

Such suspicion of the patriarchal tendency and limited spiritual viewpoint of the desert sayings yields grief that this woman, like so many other women, were deprived of their natural relationships with their male family members. And before we give into believing too readily in this woman's prompt pacification, we might recall her tenacity as a sign of wisdom and love and resistance to the emerging dominant mindset of viewing spiritual life as facilitated by the depriving of oneself and family relations, and the agreeing to this deprivation in others. Indeed, we should note that this particular story is among the many attributed to Poemen in the Alphabetical Collection (the longest section by far in the Alphabetical Collection), and yet in the Systematic Collection, it is collected in the section on Self-Control. Whose self-control is being lauded here? Is it Poemen and his brothers for having curtailed an implied desire to see their mother, a desire certainly not described at any point in the story? Or is it the mother's exemplary self-control, as she is convinced by Poemen to go away "in joy" and leave her sons in peace? Though a case might be made for each, I tend to think the second instance of "self-control" is more likely than the first. This is a self-control being taught to the early faith community by those desiring to be left alone to their own devices as they design their own spiritual paths.

Another story tells of Poemen's interaction with a sister:

> One day the magistrate of that district wanted to see Abba Poemen but the old man did not want to see him. So, he seized his sister's son and threw him into prison, under the pretext that he was a criminal saying, "If the old man comes to intercede for him I will let him go." Then his sister came to weep at Poemen's door, but he gave her no answer. Then she reproached him in these words, saying, "Heart of stone, have pity on me, for he is my only son." But he only said to her, "Poemen has not brought forth any sons." At that, she went away. When he heard this, the magistrate sent Poemen this message, "If you only ask me by a word, I will let him go." The old man replied, "Judge him according to the law; if he is worthy of death, put him to death, if not, do what you choose." (Poemen 5)

Poemen, represented by his sister as "heart of stone," shows here exemplary resistance to being manipulated by the public magistrate. The magistrate himself shows credible understanding of men's systems of fidelity in the desert by choosing to throw a nephew into jail rather than the sister. His gender and his age render the nephew of greater value than Poemen's sister and more likely to convince Poemen to bow to the magistrate's wishes. That he does not do so constitutes the central value of this story, and we could cautiously congratulate Poemen on not buying into this value system and instead standing his own ground.

However, women's ways of love are not evident in the sister's persistence in this story. She says her piece, asking for pity, recognizing that Poemen should be able to recognize the value of an only son for her and the wreck her life would be if she lost him. Poemen's response is to distance himself wholly from the relationship and to, instead, seem to call forth this woman's own power to release her son rather than rely on him. I, at first, read this story as disheartening in that Poemen represents himself as more concerned with resisting manipulation and preserving his own way of life than to get involved in public affairs that do not concern him. Reflecting further, we might also consider Poemen resisting the power relations of his time and using his refusal to get involved as a means to encourage his sister to not rely on him but on herself and, indeed, on the law. Poemen knows the magistrate cannot legitimately do the son any harm and will have to release him, so the immediacy with which his sister leaves his presence can be thought of not just as a severing of their familial relations but of being reminded of her own capacities to demand that injustices of the kind mentioned here in violent language—the son is "seized" and "thrown into" prison—be tended to. The outcome of the story, of course, remains a mystery. We never hear from Poemen's sister again, but we are left with troubling implications that could be drawn from interactions such as these concerning men's desire to withhold themselves from the families who needed them. This is a troubling sort of love, if we read as charitably as we can and see it as a desire to encourage others to get along without them.

Women on Their Own

Told to get by on their own, many women did just that. Complicit with the men's forming communities of and among themselves, stories of these women nevertheless enter the desert sayings collections as important vestiges of lives being lived in creative ways, independent of the men's presence or help. In ways, we might still harbor suspicion about these stories in that they allow men to feel satisfied that women were doing just fine without them; but, more charitably interpreted, we might also see the stories as evidence of women's vulnerabilities that, when shared, created opportunities for communal sustenance and mutual empowerment.

One story tells of a woman raped by a soldier while her mother was not at home. Having already adopted some kind of uniform that identified her as a desert daughter, though living ostensibly in an urban setting, this woman immediately removed the clothing as a symbolic act that she could no longer identify herself as an ascetic devoted to God. In addition, she grieved the event. Her position of seeming disgrace attracted the pity of many other women and of priests who urged her to take on the quasi-monastic habit she had doffed. She, however, would not let herself be persuaded, even when her visitors tried to convince her that the rape had not been her fault. Unfortunately for readers of this story, we hear her reasons for not taking on the clothing or role she had formerly held in her community: "God has cast me off," she says. "How can I put on again the habit of the God who does not want me? Could God not have prevented the affront? If he saw that I was unworthy of the habit, then so I am remaining" (Sorrow for Sin 49). She seems convinced that some inherent unworthiness has been manifested by this act of a man's toward her, and that this story is collected in a chapter on sorrow for sin could indicate the woman's desire to grieve her own sin or that of the man's. This woman's self-understanding and understanding of God, however, both appear skewed and sensitive readers will likely cringe at the outcome of this story: "Until the day she died, she continued weeping and lamenting in salutary grief with excessive sorrow for sin."

This seems a story functioning to highlight commitment and complacency. This woman accepts an act of violence toward her as evidence of what God wishes and sees it as revealing a new possibility for her: a new vocation of commitment to grief. We might regret her seeing things this way and wish that she had rather used the opportunity to pursue a more life-giving form of activity for the remainder of her days.

If the rape caused her to conceive a child, we might hope that she found some joy in pregnancy and motherhood that the desert stories could not possibly archive given their seeming focus on the ascetic life. That the woman has a community though to join her and not ostracize her, to accept her as the woman they had known all along as an ascetic, seems important. That they do not insist on their own interpretations of the man's act but let the woman voice her own experience of what has happened is an exemplary act of restraining their own violence they might have enacted against her. That we see her own attitude as a kind of self-mutilation is possible, but my suspicion is that the story carries the values of the protomonastic communities and makes space for women who grieve, for whatever reason. This representation of values could obscure what really happened in the story.

For instance, that the mother is not given voice in the story is poignant. What would we hear, if her words were remembered? The story jumps immediately from the young woman's report of what happened and then a report of the many days she grieved before visitors approached to try to console her. The mother could not have been silent during this time. That her words are omitted could indicate that they were harsh words, that she blamed her daughter for what happened. I also sense the possibility that the woman was sad for her daughter but also amazed to see what might happen as a result of this sudden disruption to the status of her daughter as a "devout virgin." Might this woman eventually have grandchildren then? Was she hopeful that her daughter's grief might turn to joy?

Another story of a woman and daughter represents them as in need of alms (Indifference to Goods 22). Some Greek visitors with money to offer were taken to their Egyptian home and the women refuse to receive alms. At first, the daughter answers the door and reports that her mother has gone to work that day so they will have food enough; they have no need of the visitors' alms. Indeed, she reports her mother's instruction to her before she left as "Cheer up," a word identical in the Greek to Jesus's "take heart" recorded in healing stories (Matt 9:2; Mark 10:49). Later, when the mother returns, the visitors again press her to receive their alms, but she persists in refusing it, claiming God is taking care of the family. To receive alms from visitors would compromise the care God offers them. The story ends reporting how the visitors "glorified God on hearing her faith." Like the story recounted in chapter 2 about the son whose mother was providentially supplied for, enabling his *not* supplying her needs and to continue to attend to his own needs, we might hear in this story a similar sensibility advanced: God is taking care of families whose men are absent. Women reading the story should expect God to take care of them, rather than male family members or male members of the community. This story operates as a pass for such men to go about their own lives, firm in the belief that women can do just fine without them. The story demonstrates women's gritty determination to respond to offers from God and to resist assistance from humans because accepting it might somehow kill the goose that laid the golden eggs.

These two stories express the poignant wish within the sayings that women might be devising their own ways of spiritual becoming with God as their benefactor and judge, and men hardly on the scene at all except to counsel and give alms. That men and women were not meant to live entirely alone is suggested by the wholesome humanity of these desert sons and daughters that persists in the stories even as the actors in them seem to want to wish the other away as a distraction to a purpose they discern God wants for them. Whether or not the raped virgin conceived, these women were mothers. As Luce Irigaray writes:

> We are always mothers just by being women. We bring many things into the world apart from children, we give

> birth to many other things apart from children: love, desire, language, art, social things, political things, religious things, but this kind of creativity has been forbidden to us for centuries. We must take back this maternal creative dimension that is our birthright as women. . . . Our task is to give life back to that mother, to the mother who lives within us and among us.[1]

This was the task of the community come to console the rape victim. This was the task of her silent mother. This was the task of the mother and daughter refusing to take alms from the visitors. My task in this book has been to give life back to the mothers who populated the Christian desert and those who remain unknown to us but whose sons and their words have taken privileged place in the Christian tradition. Though I have called such women desert daughters, my task has been to remind us of our own undiscovered dimensions of maternity, as we learn from and consider our responses to stories of both women and men, desert daughters and desert sons, in the Christian desert tradition. To note what has been missing and what we ourselves must supply.

Women's *Xeniteia*

The book ends with *xeniteia* as a wonderful metaphor for human being: voluntary exile. Not to consider the self as "finished." Not to consider the self and its "stages" of spiritual growth as useful even. Rather, to envisage the self as in self-chosen exile from the strictures within which objectification of the other confines one, or by which strictures one has been confined oneself. As Luce Irigaray writes,

---

1. Luce Irigaray, *Sexes and Genealogies,* trans. Gillian C. Gill (New York: Columbia University Press, 1993), 18.

> Going to a foreign land is not necessary in order to expro-
> priate oneself from a familiar same and uncover in this way
> what most radically is proper to self. This process can take
> place through an exile of self that a making outside oneself
> partially represents, provided that it is accompanied by a
> return to oneself.[2]

Being and letting be. The cultivation of space between the
two. Women as wanderers: as wanderers beyond themselves,
and beyond the roles that men have assigned them and they
have assigned themselves given their conditioning within a
patriarchal culture. Can we constructively appropriate a wandering beyond this form in order to liberate ourselves and find
a place of plenitude and flourishing, not just for ourselves but
for men, as well? A place beyond men's knowing, so that they
are forced to do their own wandering from the established
place their own forms of self-protection have forced them
into? Could men be forced not to pursuit of the wandering
woman, but to their own voluntary exile from the place in
which their own patriarchal and androcentric thinking places
themselves, quite without their intention or desire but places
them nevertheless? That is the hope this book expresses. John
Moschos reported an elder as teaching: "Children, salt comes
from water. But if it comes back to water, it is dissolved and
disappears. So the monk comes from a woman; and if he comes
back to a woman, he is undone and, insofar, as his being a
monk is concerned, he dies."[3]

Given the desert context this undoing of man makes sense.
The monastic vocation as it was being set up in late antiquity
relied on a certain identity marker being severance of ties to

---

2. Luce Irigaray, *The Way of Love*, trans. Heidi Bosti and Stephen
Pluháček (New York: Continuum, 2002), 89.

3. John Moschos, *The Spiritual Meadow*, trans. John Wortley, CS 139
(Kalamazoo, MI: Cistercian Publications, 1992), 193.

family and to the family a man might form with a woman. The undoing though that is suggested here within a warning by John Moschos might also be seen as a hopeful promise: that man's return to the beloved would undo any of the identity he had begun to form on his own among other men and instead render him open to being newly formed in wholesome community with others.

Bibliography

The Anonymous Sayings of the Desert Fathers: A Select Edition and Complete English Translation. Translated by John Wortley. Cambridge: Cambridge University Press, 2013.

Athanasius. *The Life of Antony.* Translated by Robert C. Gregg. Classics of Western Spirituality. New York: Paulist Press, 1980.

Basil. *Ascetical Works.* Translated by Sister M. Monica Wagner. Fathers of the Church 9. Washington, DC: Catholic University of America Press, 1962.

The Book of the Elders: Sayings of the Desert Fathers. Translated by John Wortley. CS 240. Collegeville, MN: Liturgical Press, 2012.

Brakke, David. *Demons and the Making of the Monk: Spiritual Combat in Early Christianity.* Cambridge, MA: Harvard University Press, 2006.

Brown, Peter. *The Body and Society: Men, Women, and Sexual Renunciation in Early Christianity.* New York: Columbia University Press, 1988.

———. "The Rise and Function of the Holy Man in Late Antiquity." *Journal of Roman Studies* 61 (1971): 80–101.

Burke, Kenneth. *The Philosophy of Literary Form: Studies in Symbolic Action.* 3rd ed. Berkeley: University of California Press, 1973.

Burton-Christie, Douglas. *The Word in the Desert: Scripture and the Quest for Holiness in Early Christian Monasticism.* New York: Oxford University Press, 1993.

Chitty, Derwas J. *The Desert a City: An Introduction to the Study of Egyptian and Palestinian Monasticism under the Christian Empire.* Crestwood, NY: St. Vladimir's Seminary Press, 1999.

The Chreia in Ancient Rhetoric: The Progymnasmata. Edited by Ronald F. Hock and Edward N. O'Neil. Atlanta: Scholars Press, 1986.

Clark, Elizabeth A. "The Lady Vanishes: Dilemmas of a Feminist Historian after the 'Linguistic Turn.'" *Church History* 67, no. 1 (1998): 1–31.

Cloke, Gillian. *'This Female Man of God': Women and Spiritual Power in the Patristic Age, AD 350–450*. New York: Routledge, 1995.

Connor, Alice. *Fierce: Women of the Bible and Their Stories of Violence, Mercy, Bravery, Wisdom, Sex, and Salvation*. Minneapolis, MN: Fortress, 2017.

The Desert Fathers. Translated by Helen Waddell. New York: Vintage Books, 1998.

De Wet, Chris L. "Grumpy Old Men?: Gender, Gerontology, and the Geriatrics of Soul in John Chrysostom." *Journal of Early Christian Studies* 24, no. 4 (2016): 491–521.

Dodds, E. R. *Pagan and Christian in an Age of Anxiety: Some Aspects of Religious Experience from Marcus Aurelius to Constantine*. Cambridge: Cambridge University Press, 1965.

Eilberg-Schwartz, Howard. "The Nakedness of a Woman's Voice, The Pleasure in a Man's Mouth: An Oral History of Ancient Judaism." In *Off With Her Head!: The Denial of Women's Identity in Myth, Religion, and Culture*, edited by Howard Eilberg-Schwartz and Wendy Doniger, 165–84. Berkeley: University of California Press, 1995.

Elliott, Alison Goddard. *Roads to Paradise: Reading the Lives of the Early Saints*. Hanover, NH: University Press of New England, 1987.

Elm, Susanna. *'Virgins of God': The Making of Asceticism in Late Antiquity*. Oxford: Oxford University Press, 1994.

Eucherius of Lyons. "In Praise of the Desert." Translated by Charles Cummings. In *The Lives of the Jura Fathers*, edited by Tim Vivian, Kim Vivian, and Jeffrey Burton Russell, 197–215. CS 178. Kalamazoo, MI: Cistercian Publications, 1999.

Eusebius. *The Ecclesiastical History*. Translated by J. E. L. Oulton. Cambridge, MA: Harvard University Press, 1973.

Evagrius. *The Praktikos and Chapters on Prayer*. Translated by John Eudes Bamberger. CS 4. Collegeville, MN: Cistercian Publications, 1972.

Forman, Mary. *Praying with the Desert Mothers*. Collegeville, MN: Liturgical Press, 2005.

Frank, Georgia. *The Memory of the Eyes: Pilgrims to Living Saints in Christian Late Antiquity*. Berkeley: University of California Press, 2000.

Franzmann, Majella. *Women and Religion*. New York, NY: Oxford University Press, 2000.

Give Me A Word: The Alphabetical Sayings of the Desert Fathers. Translated by John Wortley. Yonkers, NY: St. Vladimir's Seminary Press, 2014.

Gregory of Nyssa. *The Life of Moses*. Translated by Abraham J. Malherbe and Everett Ferguson. Classics of Western Spirituality. New York: Paulist Press, 1978.

Hadot, Pierre. *Philosophy as a Way of Life: Spiritual Exercises from Socrates to Foucault*. Translated by Michael Chase. Malden, MA: Blackwell, 1995.

Harmless, William. *Desert Christians: An Introduction to the Literature of Early Monasticism*. New York: Oxford University Press, 2004.

Irigaray, Luce. *In the Beginning, She Was*. New York: Bloomsbury, 2013.

———. *Sexes and Genealogies*. Translated by Gillian C. Gill. New York: Columbia University Press, 1993.

———. *The Way of Love*. Translated by Heidi Bostic and Stephen Pluháček. New York: Continuum, 2002.

Isaiah of Scetis. *Ascetic Discourses*. Translated by John Chryssavgis and Pachomios Penkett. CS 150. Kalamazoo, MI: Cistercian Publications, 2002.

John Cassian. *Institutes*. Translated by Boniface Ramsey. Ancient Christian Writers 58. Mahwah, NJ: Newman, 2000.

John Moschos. *Spiritual Meadow*. Translated by John Wortley. CS 139. Kalamazoo, MI: Cistercian Publications, 1992.

Katos, Demetrios S. *Palladius of Helenopolis: The Origenist Advocate*. Oxford: Oxford University Press, 2011.

Keller, Catherine. *Face of the Deep: A Theology of Becoming.* New York: Routledge, 2003.

Lane, Belden. "Desert Attentiveness, Desert Indifference: Countercultural Spirituality in the Desert Fathers and Mothers." *CrossCurrents* 44, no. 2 (1994): 193–206.

———. *Desert Spirituality and Cultural Resistance: From Ancient Monks to Mountain Refugees.* Eugene, OR: Wipf and Stock, 2018.

———. *The Great Conversation: Nature and the Care of the Soul.* New York: Oxford University Press, 2019.

Leloir, Louis. "Woman and the Desert Fathers." *Vox Benedictina* 3, no. 3 (1986): 207–27.

The Lives of the Desert Fathers: The Historia Monachorum in Aegypto. Translated by Norman Russell. CS 34. Kalamazoo, MI: Cistercian Publications, 1981.

"The Martyrdom of Saints Perpetua and Felicitas." In *The Acts of the Christian Martyrs*, translated by Herbert Musurillo, 106–131. Oxford: Clarendon Press, 1972.

McEntee, Rory and Adam Bucko. *New Monasticism: An Interspiritual Manifesto for Contemplative Living.* Maryknoll, NY: Orbis Books, 2015.

Merton, Thomas. *Learning to Love: Exploring Solitude and Freedom,* The Journals of Thomas Merton 6. New York: HarperCollins, 2010.

———. *The Wisdom of the Desert: Sayings of the Desert Fathers of the Fourth Century.* Boston: Shambhala, 2004.

Mobsby, Ian and Mark Berry. *A New Monastic Handbook: From Vision to Practice.* Norwich: Canterbury, 2014.

Newman, Jay. *Competition in Religious Life.* Ontario: Wilfrid Laurier University Press, 1989.

Origen. *On First Principles.* Translated by G. W. Butterworth. New York: Harper & Row, 1966.

———. *The Song of Songs: Commentary and Homilies.* Translated by R. P. Lawson. Ancient Christian Writers 26. Westminster, MD: Newman, 1957.

Palladius. *Lausiac History.* Translated by Robert T. Meyer. Ancient Christian Writers 34. Mahwah, NJ: Paulist Press, 1964.

Pseudo-Athanasius. *The Life and Regimen of the Blessed and Holy Syncletica.* Translated by Elizabeth Bryson Bongie. Eugene, OR: Wipf and Stock, 2005.

Rapp, Claudia. *Holy Bishops in Late Antiquity: The Nature of Christian Leadership in an Age of Transition.* Berkeley: University of California Press, 2005.

Regnault, Lucien. *The Day-to-Day Life of the Desert Fathers.* Translated by Étienne Poirier, Jr. Petersham, MA: St. Bede's Publications, 1998.

The Sayings of the Desert Fathers: The Alphabetical Collection. Translated by Benedicta Ward. CS 59. Kalamazoo, MI: Cistercian Publications, 1984.

Schneiders, Sandra M. "A Hermeneutical Approach to the Study of Christian Spirituality." In *Minding the Spirit: The Study of Christian Spirituality,* edited by Elizabeth A. Dreyer and Mark S. Burrows, 49–60. Baltimore, MD: Johns Hopkins University Press, 2005.

Schüssler Fiorenza, Elisabeth. *Wisdom Ways: Introducing Feminist Biblical Interpretation.* Maryknoll, NY: Orbis Books, 2001.

Sheldrake, Philip. "Spirituality and Its Critical Methodology." In *Exploring Christian Spirituality: Essays in Honor of Sandra M. Schneiders, IHM,* edited by Bruce H. Lescher and Elizabeth Liebert, 15–34. Mahwah, NJ: Paulist Press, 2006.

Špidlík, Tomaš. *Prayer: The Spirituality of the Christian East.* CS 206. Kalamazoo, MI: Cistercian Publications, 2005.

Stewart, Columba. "The Portrayal of Women in the Sayings and Stories of the Desert." *Vox Benedictina* 2, no. 1 (1985): 5–23.

———. "'We'?: Reflections on Affinity and Dissonance in Reading Early Monastic Literature." *Spiritus* 1, no. 1 (2001): 93–102.

———. *Working the Earth of the Heart: The Messalian Controversy in History, Texts, and Language to A.D. 431.* Oxford: Clarendon Press, 1991.

Swan, Laura. *The Forgotten Desert Mothers: Sayings, Lives, and Stories of Early Christian Women.* Mahwah, NJ: Paulist Press, 2001.

Thomas of Celano. "The Remembrance of the Desire of a Soul." In *Francis of Assisi: Early Documents Volume Two: the Founder,* edited by Regis J. Armstrong, J. A. Wayne Hellmann, and William J. Short, 239–393. New York: New City Press, 2000.

Ward, Benedicta. *Harlots of the Desert: A Study of Repentance in Early Monastic Sources.* CS 106. Kalamazoo, MI: Cistercian Publications, 1987.

Wilson-Hartgrove, Jonathan. *The Wisdom of Stability: Rooting Faith in a Mobile Culture.* Brewster, MA: Paraclete, 2010.